# PETALS OF DISTINCTION

## ROSIE HARTWIG-BENSON

Jan-Carol
Publishing, Inc
"every story needs a book"

Petals of Distinction
Rosie Hartwig-Benson
Published November 2017
Express Editions
Imprint of Jan-Carol Publishing, Inc
Copyright © 2017 Rosie Hartwig-Benson
Photography: Rosie Hartwig-Benson

ISBN: 978-1-945619-46-5
Library of Congress Control Number: 2017960367

You may contact the publisher:
Jan-Carol Publishing, Inc
PO Box 701
Johnson City, TN 37605
publisher@jancarolpublishing.com
jancarolpublishing.com

This book honors the memory of my treasured parents and is dedicated to my precious son; my gift from God.

I love you more than words can express.

# AUTHOR'S NOTE

I realize there is a lesson in everything we face. When self-doubt whispered through the fog of my pain, I was blessed to observe signs of His presence. I remembered what is possible. During those moments, I knew I was to share my pilgrimage.

Each day is a gift. Stop and contemplate how amazing life is. Make memories. May you find inspiration on your journey by allowing your faith to be the radar that sees you through the fog.

*—Rosie*

# FOREWORD

After forty years in medicine most physicians feel that they have seen everything possible concerning the human condition. I can tell you that I have never experienced a patient like Rose. The story of her personal medical journey is compelling to me and should be insightful to anyone struggling with any chronic disease. She recounts the disappointment of delay and incorrect diagnosis and yet never became bitter at the limitations of her physicians. She painstakingly takes the reader through the agonies of treatment, complications of surgeries, and the true despair of grieving those losses, as well as the personal losses of her loved ones. This story will bolster the discouraged to lean on their faith, friends, and physicians to move forward one day at a time. Never alone.

—Edward M. Beadle, M.D.
*Fellow of the American College of Obstetricians and Gynecologists*

# CONTENTS

# IS THERE LIFE
# BEYOND THIS?

L ife can be unpredictable. One agonizing morning in June of 1998, lying motionless in a hospital bed, a storm of rough waters was stirring within me. I awoke with a jarring awareness: if I were to disconnect from the nutritional tubing attached to me, it would put an end to my suffering.

It was two weeks after a life-altering surgery. Listening to the whirl of machines and beeping monitors that were keeping my malnourished body of a mere eighty pounds alive was unsettling. My thoughts were exploding with apprehension of how I would survive a lifetime of not eating orally.

The brash alarm of the feeding pump was blaring nonstop due to an air bubble. A mix of the physical pain and emotional toll coursed through me. Instead of pressing the call button, my trembling hand reached over and shut off the clamorous machine. I felt an absence of hope in knowing how to conquer this new life battle of tubal maintenance, hunger pangs, pain levels, and immobility. The angst and emptiness of the emaciated body of my former self were inescapable. This new existence was not the future I had envisioned in my dreams.

A doctor strode into the room. He noticed the intravenous therapy was infusing, but surprise registered on his face when he detected the nutritional therapy wasn't running.

I told him in a pathetic voice, "I shut off the machine because I needed a break." I locked onto his soulful eyes, which radiated empathy. They seemed to plead, *Rosie, don't give up.* He stayed by my side for what seemed like hours, although in reality only 8–10 minutes ticked by on the wall clock.

A seasoned nurse entered the room and adjusted the pump settings. The machine squealed when the nutritional formula started infusing. The doctor asked her to please close the door behind her when she left to give us privacy. When the door closed, a sinking feeling of entrapment made me quiver due to the overwhelming situation of machines keeping me alive and immobilization. He sat down and asked me about my home life. I told him I was yearning to see my eleven-year-old son.

I asked him to please open the mail on the bedside table. He agreed and read a note from my son aloud.

"Dear Mom, I love you very much. I hope your surgery went okay. I hope the people at the hospital are taking good care of you. You will have a lot to tell me when you get home, if you can. I love you."

Nestled inside the envelope was a precious photograph of him.

I gave a sigh of bliss to have had this letter read to me and to view the photo of my son's endearing grin. It was a four-hour round-trip commute for my family to drive to visit me at the hospital. Work schedules didn't allow for this luxury to happen too often. Phone conversations were rare and brief, because I was too feeble to hold the phone receiver.

Before the doctor left my bedside, he asked, "Rosie, would you allow a lady to come and sit with you?" I agreed. Within minutes, a lady chaplain entered my room. She had a pleasant smile, and comforting softness in her voice. She anointed me with Holy water and read from Isaiah 43:1–2:

"I, the Lord, created you. Fear not: for I have called you by name; now you belong to me. When you cross deep rivers, I will be with you, when you walk through fire, I will be with you. To me, you are very dear and I love you. Don't be afraid, for I am with you."

In my solitude, it was not about the odds, or the relentless pain of my wounds. It became about my willpower, and finding the strength to see the light of a new day. Could I reach into my inner soul and unlock more determination?

The next morning, the first task was to try to lift my weak head off of the pillow. Two nurses assisted me in swinging my legs to the side of the bed, putting one foot down on the floor and then the other. I attempted my first tentative steps while holding on to a walker for support. A nurse moving the machines attached to me expressed encouragement. Through painful perseverance, I continued to take one step at a time until the room seemed to be moving around and around, and then everything went black.

I awoke in throbbing pain to see a dark-haired man with gentle eyes by my side, checking my pulse. I thought I was dreaming, because he was the best eye candy I had seen by my bedside. In a joking manner, he told me he was the janitor. His delightful sense of humor was refreshing, and induced laughter helped me sparkle like a splash of water in sunlight. It was painful to laugh, although essential for my well-being. This buoyant man went on to tell me he was doing an internship at the hospital, and had assisted the surgeon during my surgery.

The following days were consumed with harrowing attempts to wake up and strengthen my body through bedside occupational and physical therapy. I was filled with new affirmations of a life so full of overbearing pain, enfeeblement, and hunger I knew only God could carry me through.

After twenty-one days of being hospitalized, I begged not to be transferred to a nursing care facility; I wanted to go home to my son. I was permitted to be released from the hospital and arrangements were made for me to have home health care. Soon I would be en route to the main reason I was fighting to stay alive: my young son, who needed his mother.

Once I was placed into the car to go home, I knew deep down in my heart the struggles were just beginning. The pain was intense, and mixed with the nauseating sense of a world in motion. I was starting to realize the end was near, no matter how much determination was stirring within me.

During the grueling car ride, I told myself, *Hold on. You will see the light of your life in a few more miles.* I asked the driver to please stop the car along a side street. I was throwing up bile, and needed the car door open for fresh air to circulate the stale air trapped in the car. My world was spinning from dehydration. I was drained and prayed for God to help me maintain.

When the car proceeded into the driveway, I realized maybe begging to

3

come home was a mistake. How in the world could I get up a flight of stairs and into bed?

My dear son ran to embrace me. His welcome home hug and kiss were heavenly medicine. The loving concern etched on his face made my determination to endure grow to new levels.

Once in bed, my breathing became labored. I remember hearing garbled voices and swaying images. The rescue squad had entered my bedroom because a family member had called 911. Communication between the EMTs was frantic; they asked relatives in the room questions about my medical conditions.

I saw dazzling light above me; following the glow, I seemed light as air while floating into total brightness. Loving warmth saturated with a peacefulness I had *never* experienced before bathed and caressed me. I wanted to keep following the harmonious tranquility. I also felt myself struggling to go back to my son who was next to my bedside holding my hand. Or was my mother holding my hand? My vision was blanketed by pure whiteness. I was searching to find my son, but also seeking the journey to heaven. At this juncture, I was caught between two worlds. I heard a voice say, "Take some deep, even breaths, Rosie." I felt myself being lifted back onto the mattress. Heaven was put on hold.

Several hours passed, and my body was screaming in amplified pain. I whispered, "Why, Lord, must I live in anguish when I have now felt your peace?" I recall the absence of any sound in the room except the hum of the machines helping to keep me stable and restore hydration. I wept in the stillness with indescribable fatigue.

The next weeks were a whirlwind of unabated pain, fevers and chills, palpitations, intravenous therapy, and jejunal tube feeding. It was a shock when my gaze into a mirror unveiled a skeletal, pale-faced lady with sunken, hollow, green eyes looking back at me. I observed two tubes coming out of her abdomen and an intravenous line in her wrist, fingers rigid and curled. To comprehend that it was me was very woeful.

In case God was about to whisper "It is time to come home," I made some final arrangements with my pastor. I instructed a girlfriend to type my composed inner thoughts to my son in a keepsake letter to him. My church grandma was asked to locate and print the lyrics to the song "Sweet, Sweet Spirit" for my request to be sung. I am an organized soul, and wanted things in order. I was ready for heaven's peace.

My body seemed to be shutting down. I was taken by ambulance to the hospital and admitted with abnormal heart rhythms, critical potassium levels, and dehydration complications.

A few days later, I fell when trying to get myself to the bathroom and I could not get up. Feeling helpless and powerless, I wished for the world of pain and weakness to come to a halt. I prayed for a sea of calmness to enter my surroundings and flow through my overtaxed body.

I recalled a line from one of my favorite poems: "My precious child, I love you and will never leave you during your trials and testing. When you see only one set of footprints it is then that I am carrying you."

God sees when a sparrow falls; surely He was carrying me, helping me to be steadfast. I adamantly resolved to stay alive for my son.

# SEEKING
# ANSWERS

In a blink of an eye, everything can change. The spring of 2017 marked the twenty-year anniversary of surviving the odds of not consuming food orally, along with accepting the challenges of only taking a few sips of water to swish and spit in order to coat my parched mouth. These taxing issues resulted in life-threatening conditions of malnutrition and dehydration, with chronic health consequences.

It was an arduous task in the 1970s, 1980s, and 1990s to find help in unveiling my overloaded case of perplexing symptoms. I have been in more critical care emergency facilities, hospitals, and surgical areas than I care to remember. At times my challenging health issues baffled doctors, and my name became synonymous with the term unique. It has taken most of my life for my complex medical mystery to be diagnosed and treated.

I have been blessed with skilled surgeons, physicians, specialists, and nurses. I thank them for their caring assistance, from the bottom of my heart. No professor or textbook is able to teach you how to sympathize with a patient. Genuine bedside kindness is never antiquated.

I have also had my share of physicians who looked at me, mystified, and articulated, "What the hell?" Others stated, tentatively, "Anorexia?" These statements left me feeling dispirited, especially when I was also asked, "Are you sure you don't drink too much?" I would explain I had never been a drinker of spirits, caffeinated sodas, or any type of coffee.

During the extended years of seeking answers, I kept declining and eventually lost 100 pounds. I was in debilitating pain, malnourished, and dehydrated. I struggled to breathe while bedridden. Being malnourished and dehydrated with electrolyte imbalances affects my whole body, causing complicated uncertainty to the next endeavor in survival.

I constantly went from having one medical procedure or test to the next. I continued to suffer a plethora of symptoms. I researched my conditions in earnest to help find an answer, and finally discovered a disease with relevant symptoms that hit home.

At my next clinical appointment, I importuned for more testing. "I have all of the symptoms of celiac disease," I explained. "I can't keep food down. I have chronic fatigue, joint pain, anemia, abdominal bloating, vomiting, diarrhea then constipation, skin lesions, weight loss, mouth ulcers, blisters, infertility, and depression."

I was referred to gastroenterologists, who arranged to have me go through another endoscopy. The doctor took a biopsy of my small intestine, and the pathologist identified and confirmed I did indeed have celiac disease (CD). At last, the medical diagnosis was revealed—in 1996. I wish I could have been given this result when I was preschool age and the first symptoms appeared.

Celiac disease is not a food allergy or intolerance; it is a serious auto-immune disease. A genetic predisposition evoked an immune-mediated response to gluten exposure throughout my body, with inflammation and damage to the intestinal lining. Other parts of my body were also affected. Abnormal functioning of my immune system produced antibodies against my own tissues. I was unlucky enough to have this predisposition since birth and feel the classification of a "wasting away disease" is correct.

I went on a strict diet of gluten-free food: no wheat, barley, or rye. Oats, corn, and lactose products were also eliminated. After years of suffering, I felt confident that in time, my health would become stable. I didn't realize the complexity of my situation; maybe no one did at that time.

Researching further, I found various hidden names lurking in products as gluten. Implementing end of the month billing meant licking hundreds of postage stamps and envelopes, which in turn would make me ill. I discovered the glue adhesive was made with wheat starch, which contains gluten. This was before self-adhesive stamps and envelopes were available at my employment.

I would return home from church on Sunday morning and suddenly be spewing. The communion wafer was found to be the culprit. Just one tiny wafer each communion was enough to cause continuing distress. Products I used daily were depositing poison into my system. Certain shampoos made my scalp burn and bleed. Lipstick and lip balm caused oral ulcers due to hidden gluten, listed in the ingredients as hydrolyzed wheat protein. A bit of gluten swallowed from the use of toothpaste introduced more poison into my system, causing more symptoms and additional suffering.

The plain and simple fact is that gluten is poisonous to my system. I had been infested with the evil molecule, infecting me through my unawareness of gluten in so many products, and years of being misdiagnosed. My body couldn't withstand it any longer, and was weeping with debilitating symptoms. It was much like having a stomach flu virus each and every day of my life, chronically draining me with disorders my body couldn't tolerate anymore. It felt like my whole being was in acute distress.

After months of eliminating gluten-containing grains and products, I became disheartened—my health was still not being restored. I was told by a physician, "You shouldn't be sick if you are following the diet." After listening to that statement, I sat there dumbfounded. I was faithful in navigating a gluten-free diet, and militant against any cross-contamination in a world filled with gluten. I wanted desperately to feel better. Instead, I was still weak and limp, like a wet noodle.

Testing, evaluations, and numerous clinic visits seemed never-ending. Trying to add a bit of amusement to the complexity, I clipped a medical cartoon out of the newspaper and showed it to the gastroenterologist. The understanding doctor laughed after reading the cartoon, and he praised me for keeping a sense of humor. The ability to find jocularity despite my unyielding circumstances was a real survival instinct. I underwent yet more testing, in hopes of disclosing solutions.

After unremitting abdominal pain, bloating, and persistent pelvic pain manifested, my team of doctors found it a necessity to take the unusual step of exploratory laparotomy in the autumn of 1996. I consented to the procedure. They discovered chronic cholecystitis, gallstones, ulcers, and a pelvic cyst with several loops of bowel wrapped around it. I was hospitalized for two weeks in Minneapolis. It wasn't a pleasant experience going through recovery with a long abdominal incision, staple stitches, pelvic sutures, and endless spewing.

Months after that surgery, I was still ill. The scale revealed more and more weight loss, until doctors stated, "We are losing you, Rosie. Try eating more, we are losing you." Eat *more?* I had been expressing for quite some time that despite heroic efforts at trying to eat small amounts of ground food or drink liquid supplementation, I was not able to keep anything down. I would always suffer the immediate ramifications of being ill, spending the rest of the day in the bathroom with postprandial pain.

I wept in despair, with no one to hold me except God. My life and body were in non-functioning order. I felt adrift on dry land, in utter disarray.

I had gone from severe to chronic to life-threatening. I was bedridden around the clock, due to exhaustion and depletion of nutrients.

Specialists referred me to the world-famous Mayo Clinic in Rochester, Minnesota the spring of 1997. When I entered Mayo, I felt I became a number—not a human being with a name. The waiting room reminded me of an airport terminal. Chairs were connected together, with hundreds of people all waiting for their patient number to be announced over the intercom so they could see a specialist. I must admit, it was more than interesting to people watch. I lingered there for hours in anticipation, anxious for my number to be called. When the doctors' assistant announced, "One sixty-four," I felt like yelling out *Bingo!*

I was escorted into a small room where a doctor read over my medical files, listened to my medical journey, and set up testing for another day. Testing would involve several days and more waiting. After the consult, it was a three-hour return trip home. A few days later, I was en route back to Rochester for evaluation to begin.

The first diagnostic test on the docket was a five-hour gastric emptying study. I was to consume scrambled eggs mixed with radioactive pellets. Eggs of any type had never been pleasing to my palate. I gave myself a pep talk to prepare for the challenge.

9

When the plate of watery eggs was placed in front of me, I was reluctant to reach for the fork. I begrudgingly took the first bite and grimaced. The young x-ray assistant's eye caught my expression. She snickered to the other technician, "Watch her. Of course she wouldn't be able to get any eggs down: anorexia."

Overhearing her tactless remark, I thought *Somewhere on my chart it should state that the patient's sense of hearing is 100%.* I maintained my polite equilibrium in spite of the rising tide of raw emotions threatening to overcome me and was proud of myself for showing restraint.

I took another bite while hot tears pricked my eyes. I said a prayer for God to help me get the rest of those horrible egg pellets swallowed, and for the testing to reveal what was wrong with me. Every hour they would take a scan to determine how fast the food was leaving my stomach. I was ill after eating and spent the rest of the time I wasn't having a scan in the restroom. I have no idea how any eggs or radioactive pellets were left inside of me. I recall a receptionist coming into the ladies' room, asking if she could give me assistance. She proceeded to balance a limp rag-doll and wheeled me in for another scan.

After days of various types of testing, they discovered my Celiac disease was unresponsive to diet and had caused severe damage to my small intestine, stripping all of the villi. Testing revealed I had gastric dysmotility with severe gastroparesis, and superior mesenteric artery syndrome.

Simple terms: my stomach was and still is paralyzed. The stomach cannot empty itself of food in a normal fashion. Enzymes that should be in my saliva to start dissolving food, giving the digestive processes a boost, were also decreased or not there at all. This is one of the related symptoms of Sjogren's syndrome.

I was diagnosed with severe iron, potassium, folic acid, and vitamin D deficiencies as well as fluid retention around my heart, anemia, fibromyalgia, chronic fatigue syndrome, Raynaud's syndrome, and sleep deprivation.

Last but not least, the testing revealed I did *not* have anorexia. Proof I was correct, but would it have mattered if I was anorexic? No one should be disrespected, especially by medical professionals, with disparaging remarks concerning any condition.

I was overwhelmed hearing all of these discoveries. Vibrations of gratitude stirred within me along with praises for medical answers being revealed.

I sighed with relief to be in the car heading home, leaving the medical world behind me. In reality, it was only beginning.

*******

Major changes occurred when I arrived home. Within a few days, I was en route to a hospital in Minneapolis. A Hickman central venous catheter leading into the main artery of my heart was surgically placed to receive the type of nutritional support called total parenteral nutrition. TPN is the feeding of a person intravenously, bypassing the usual process of eating and digestion. It is administered when *no* significant nutrition is obtained by other routes. I was wasting away, and had no other choice but to find the courage to face the minute-to-minute daily risks to stay alive.

Coming out of my chest was a double-lumen catheter where the solution of TPN was connected. The lipid emulsion was infused over the course of several hours. This treatment was non-stop for six months. The most common complication is an infection of the catheter, and severe infection can cause death. For those reasons, everything needed to be precise and sterile.

The Hickman venous catheter could move out of position in my vein if I coughed, vomited, or made a minimal lifting movement. It was lying on sensitive nerve endings and shooting rocketing pain. Being unable to take oral pain medication, my tolerance was tested to the limit. It was beyond challenging for me to withstand.

I received home health care nursing assistance to start the infusion and then the nurse would leave my home. I was alone in a world I knew nothing about. I graduated from college with a degree in design and merchandising, *not* nursing. I admit I was scared during those grueling hours of lying flat while my limp body tried to absorb the solution. My body was being introduced to a new way of nourishment. I was fast being taught lessons in how strong I could be in the midst of pain, fear, and hunger. The taste, smell, and physical fullness requirements are not met with TPN. I was still experiencing hunger, despite the fact that my body was being nourished.

Focusing on a wall plaque, I read it aloud. "If you have faith as a grain of mustard seed; nothing shall be impossible unto you." I needed to relinquish my fear and trust God to guide me, giving Him the steering wheel. In the days to come, I navigated how to be my own nurse. I learned how to manage sterile occlusive dressings, how to fill syringes for saline-heparin locks after infusions, and how to administer them. All angles of my everyday needs were as skilled as possible, done to the best of my ability.

After several intense hours of infusion, I would pray for my hands to be steady enough to accomplish administering the follow-up drugs. The heparin flush would keep my line open, and the blood from clotting in the catheter.

Because a portion of the catheter was external, no more baths were permitted, no swimming, and no hot tubs. This was the start of not being able to enjoy a relaxing, candle-lit bath for meditation. I missed soaking in a bath almost as much as being able to drink and eat. It was very difficult to get dressed; finding suitable attire when leaving the house was exhausting. None of my pullover clothing was made for the apparatus of the tubing now attached to my chest.

The 3000-milliliter nutrition bag hung from a five-foot IV pole with wheels on the bottom. If I desired to inhale fresh air, I had to somehow manage to get the pole with the heavy fluid bag attached to me down a flight of stairs. I knew that even being strong-willed; I could not do this by myself. I felt trapped in my own home, and had to rely on others for help.

During an infrequent stroll with my son, I waved to a girlfriend when she drove by in her car. She later called me and said, "Rose, I didn't see a person next to the pole until I saw you wave. It hurt me to see you so frail and thin. I hope you gain strength soon."

The pole served two purposes: holding the bag of fluid, and as something for me to hold, supporting my malnourished body and keeping me from falling face forward.

On those rare occasions when someone would help me escape from my too-familiar surroundings, I handled all of the awkward, double-take glances well. It did, however, crush my heart when my health conditions had leaked outside of the walls of our home, with rumors that I was perhaps near heaven's gate.

My son had to face all of this anguish with me each waking minute. Being school age, he was faced with insensitive questions thrown at him by classmates and school authorities. They did not understand the delicate human emotions of having a confirmed ailing mother, presumed to be on her deathbed. It changed our private family life into full-blown traumatic devastation.

I continued searching for different avenues to heighten and delight my usable senses. I would try to muster up the strength to prepare healthy meals for my son as often as possible. When mealtime arrived, sitting at the table with him was helpful for a sense of normalcy. Even though I was hungry yet could not eat, I found I was able to enjoy the fragrant aromas. This was an enormous epiphany for me. We would talk about his day and our dreams. Our reward was found in being together, no matter the struggles. There is always grace in finding thankful blessings.

A new ailment occurred later, when my leg became ulcerated. I had a wound of raw flesh the size of the palm of my hand on my right leg. What a nightmare of wound care treatments it took for the ulceration to heal. I had to keep my leg elevated and limit weight-bearing, straining my already burdensome limitations. Healing took a year, for complete closure of the weeping wound.

Redness and flushing started occurring on my face. I was embarrassed when physicians and friends asked if I was wearing too much blush. I would try to make light of my burning facial skin, saying, "My mother did change my name from April Ann to Rose Ann after viewing my rosy complexion when I was born. My rosy glow is very evident today." The redness formed a butterfly shape across my nose and cheeks. The cause was found to be inflammation in various parts of my body, along with low-grade fever, achiness, and extreme fatigue.

I was again suffering from skin lesions that would itch, burn, and bleed. Those irritating blisters began at the age of five, with the culprit only being diagnosed years later: celiac disease. I recall sitting at my desk in first grade, with the teacher and classmates concerned over my elbows and knees bleeding. After school, I would go home and beg my mother to let me wear long sleeves and pants instead of short-sleeved tops and skirts. That wasn't the answer, unfortunately. My covered skin seemed to burst forth in more oozing blisters, with visible blood on my clothing. After eating lunch, exercising in gym class would cause my skin to erupt from exertion. I would be peppered from my head to my toes with an itchy rash and sensations like I was going to faint and spew. This was a fierce battle all through my school years. No one had ever heard of gluten allergies or celiac disease affecting and debilitating your health when I was a child in small-town USA.

Trying to be strong and endure all my symptoms every second of each day was taking a toll on me. Tremendous pain levels were out of control, and the effects were running rampant throughout my whole body. Being able to produce and release tears was an actual blessing of healing waters, as nothing seemed to be working to keep me nourished.

In the summer of 1998, I was referred by specialists to highly-regarded surgeons in Minneapolis for what I call my life-altering enterostomy surgery, with the medical name Janeway jejunostomy and gastrostomy placement.

Learning how to cope with survival methods of multiple stoma openings and the maintenance of tubes coming out of my abdomen was no small labor of stamina. Being bedridden and still finding the inner strength to be a full-time devoted mother and wife was a daunting task. I tried to continue to take care of my family and manage a household, when I didn't even have the nutritional support level to raise my head from the pillow to navigate out of bed.

Never in my wildest imagination had I considered what the appearance of an open hole on the left side of my abdomen, and a section of bowel lying on the right side of my abdomen, would resemble in appearance. I learned maintenance of a gastrostomy tube for the release of bile drainage, and a jejunostomy tube for continuous formula nutritional feedings. An enteral feeding pump ensured the correct amount of liquid was administered to my body over the course of a day. The enteral pump would malfunction often, leaving me with no means to receive nutrition until a new pump was ordered and delivered. My body still doesn't tolerate bolus feedings.

Even with the tubes in proper placement, both stomas leaked my inner body fluids. I wasn't absorbing enough to keep myself hydrated—or to survive. The liquid would stream down my tummy and saturate my clothing. Stoma care specialists tried to assist. Skin barriers didn't provide enough protection to keep my raw skin from breaking due to continued leakage. To say the least, I was overwhelmed with the frustration of a life turned upside down.

Upon examination, the surgeon told me, "Rosie, nothing is one hundred percent perfect." This accurate statement is prevalent yet today. Absorption and leakage issues persist.

Out of necessity, other measures needed to take place. A Port-a-Cath was surgically implanted under my skin, in the upper chest under the clavicle bone. It felt and appeared as a large bump. The port served for needle insertion for intravenous fluids and blood draws. Similar to the Hickman venous catheter years previous, this port also put pressure on sensitive nerve endings, causing unrelenting pain, misery, and more suffering.

I concentrated on my young son, mediating, and dreaming of nature and colorful sunsets while bedridden. It was my job to find more inner fortitude, allowing His light to shine forth in guiding and holding me on this painful, yet remarkable journey of survival.

Concerned friends and physicians asked, "How are you able to smile through all of this?" I replied, "God is carrying me." My mindset was and still is to embrace being called unique while thriving to survive. Putting on a determined game face has become my ultimate goal. Keeping a smile on my face was and still is indeed a victory with each new onset of challenges.

*******

While photographing a glass art piece, sunbeams streamed a kaleidoscope of colors. Viewing the bright array of hues evoked memories of overhead lights and pain while in an emergency room setting. I had been taken by ambulance to the hospital. Testing revealed my second implanted Port-a-Cath had become infected. Poison was running rampant through my bloodstream.

The life-threatening infection meant three weeks of a daily IV treatment regimen in an emergency room setting. Each session lasted six hours, with high doses of strong antibiotics being fed into my body intravenously. During the first week of treatment, I became allergic to the antibiotics administered. The high-risk infection and allergic reaction made my body weep in weakness. An itchy rash covered my entire body. I could not move my muscles to walk or get dressed. I had to have someone clothe me. By means of a wheelchair, I was taken from my home to the hospital for the treatment sessions to continue. I was in misery, yet again fighting for my life and finding the will to survive.

Lying in the emergency room on a hard gurney, strong antibiotics whirled, blending the mixture of medicines to help my weakened body eradicate the fierce infection. My fragile body felt weary. My mother was allowed entrance to check on me. She expressed to me that she was struggling with how she was going to be joyful at a family wedding that afternoon, without

15

my attendance. Tears trickled down her face as she realized just how ill I was; she did not want to be gone from my side. We prayed together before she gave me a kiss and with reluctance, departed.

Within an hour of her departure, I saw a vision of my Heavenly Father by the foot of the hospital bed protecting me. The sacredness in His eyes penetrated a calming, inner-reassurance that He is always surrounding and holding me, no matter how I may feel when my health situations are grim. I was able to close my eyes to rest while the strong antibiotics continued infusing. I felt blessed. My soul interlocked with His immense love caressing me.

After weeks of antibiotics, the surgical removal of the port was scheduled. This procedure was performed without the use of anesthesia. The magnitude of that pain was more severe than it should have been, because my body was brutally sore before the procedure ever began.

Pain levels were out of control when I heard a familiar voice drifting from the recovery room reception area. A nurse brought my devoted mother into the room to be with me. I will always remember her forlorn expressions when she saw me. She cried, saying, "I don't understand why you have to go through so much pain in your life. You fight so hard to stay alive, and you do it with such grace. I hope you know how much I love you. You bless my life, Sweet Pea." My maternal grandfather had bestowed upon me this special nickname when I was a baby. Sweet pea is the designated birth flower for the month of April, my birth month.

During the follow-up exam, I was told I would never be able to get another port implanted. Due to the severity of not one, but two port infections, it could cause swelling of my brain.

I have discovered the best portion of my life is the small nameless moments that I spend smiling with someone who matters to me. I adore when my son or friends have the ability to make me laugh when I don't even have the strength to raise my head from the pillow.

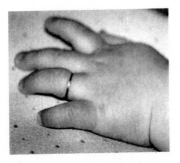

# MOTHERHOOD

On a beautiful spring afternoon, I heard in the distance of my mind a baby crying. I marked it on the calendar. In my heart, I knew it was God letting me be part of the miracle of life of my yet unseen baby. I had already gone through the steps in the adoption process. A file with my name and information was in some overfilled filing cabinet, waiting for this gift from God to arrive. I knew this was a sign I would be a mother soon. I danced around the room, inhaling the refreshing scent of lilacs drifting through open windows. The gift of hearing this distant cry penetrated deeply, suffusing me with inner happiness and warmth.

After waiting over seven years for the adoption agency to notify me, I was suddenly overflowing with adrenaline, impatient to be a mother. Whenever the phone rang, my heart would skip a beat in anticipation of the special call that would change my life.

The nursery walls were wallpapered and accented with a teddy bear border. An oak crib was assembled. Coordinating crib sheets, blankets, supplies, and clothes were purchased. My mother sewed eyelet curtains, and hand stitched a keepsake prayer plaque. Some days I had to keep the door to this attractive nursery closed. I couldn't handle the pain of seeing the crib empty. I yearned for my child to arrive, but accepted the situation with equanimity most days.

I attended months of adoption classes, filled out papers upon papers, and had several intense, personal one-on-one interviews. During this time, I am sure I saw every female in the entire universe who was pregnant. This made me feel empty. I wondered if those individuals had to experience the humiliating emotions of having their fingerprints taken to see if they were qualified applicants in becoming parents. I knew it was a necessary avenue for protection, but I felt violated with that step in the adoption process. It made for another piercing blow on top of the unfortunate consequences of being unable to conceive naturally.

My girlfriends and family members became parents. I was happy for them. My heart longed for the day I would be a mother. I was blessed and grateful when my brother and friends bestowed upon me the treasured privilege of being godmother for their children. I also spent much of my life caring for and spending quality time with my adorable nieces, who each have part of my name in theirs. I cherished creating precious lifelong memories with them when they arrived to spend weekends and summers.

Within 40 days of hearing that distant echo of a baby's cry, I decided to go home during a noon lunch break from my job. I heard my phone ringing when unlocking the front door. Thinking it was probably a telemarketer, I half-heartedly said, "Hello." Much to my shock and delight, it was a social worker, who said, "Rosie, you are a mother, to a sweet baby boy!" I was elated, overcome with emotion; I wept with thankfulness when I hung up the phone. Raw emotions cascaded down my face with the tears, revealing the overwhelming jubilation of dreams becoming reality. Tears may well be the body's way of restoring emotional equilibrium. God also blessed my husband to be home for the exuberant news of becoming parents. We quickly made arrangements to travel the next day to bring our son home.

I embraced the welcoming rain droplets rippling upon my soft skin when heading back to work. I trembled with excitement. I must have been glowing the rest of the day. I didn't tell my mother or anyone else about my motherhood phone call. I wanted to surprise everyone once I was holding my son in my arms. After work, I was thrilled to place necessary baby items—car seat, diaper bag, and so on—in the vehicle to be ready for travel the next morning. I didn't sleep that night. I was flying in the clouds with excitement. The stars twinkled like never before.

Having my son placed into my longing, loving arms was dreamlike. It was an angelic moment. Morning sunbeams streamed through the windowpanes and illuminated the warm blessing of this perfect baby boy. I noticed his stunning eyes and abundance of hair along with the pleasant scent of his skin. My heart was aflutter. Joyful tears trickled down my crimson cheeks with the realization that I was now indeed a mother. I thought he was the cutest baby in the whole wide world. He was sucking on a blue pacifier. I tenderly removed the pacifier to see his tiny heart-shaped lips. He smiled. I had never witnessed a more radiant smile in my life. His smile revealed that he knew I was his mother, and seemed to say, "What took you so long to get here, Mommy?" That once-in-a-lifetime moment was captured by a camera. Our keepsake mother and child photograph was placed in a special frame, with the caption loved. Viewing our smiles has brightened each of my days since.

The icing on this glorious moment was to find out he had been born on the date I had marked on the calendar, the day God allowed and blessed my open spirit to be so in tune with him that I heard his distant birth cry.

En route home, the first person I called was my mother. I will always recall stopping at a phone booth to place the call. (Yes, this was in the days before cellular phones.) When she heard the words, "You have a grandson," she was euphoric.

The drive home was a pure delight with the delicate cargo on board. I sat in the back seat with my son next to me in his car seat. I could not take my eyes off of his handsome face and perfect features. It was the best fairy-tale ending. The entire bundle of overwhelming emotions during this long and difficult journey was now settling into happiness. When I was at my lowest, God was planning something magnificent for me. I rejoiced to be so blessed.

When we pulled into our driveway, we noticed a flashing yard sign welcoming us, displaying the message, Congratulations, it's a Boy! My mother later realized she had left the wall phone dangling to place the sign in our yard before we arrived home. What an act of absolute love.

God is good in supplying our needs. I thank Him several times a day for the special gift He has bestowed upon me: my son. I am eternally grateful and blessed that God helped someone choose adoption and not abortion.

I recall from early childhood never wanting anything more than I wanted to be a mother: to have someone to love and care for unconditionally. The winding path in becoming a mother has been a difficult journey. I have overcome colossal obstacles. Years previously, I suffered an acute abdominal catastrophe involving emergency surgery for the removal of a ruptured ovarian tumor; it was as big as a grapefruit. Another emergency surgery arose a few months later due to severe endometriosis, requiring the removal of my uterus: an abdominal hysterectomy. I awoke from surgery with intense burning sensations from my head to my toes. I was later informed that both of my ovaries had also been removed. Induced surgical menopause symptoms were occurring immediately because of that. When the hot flashes didn't subside, I wanted to press the call button for the nurse, and yell over the intercom, "Help me! I can't find the menopause stop button on the remote!" There was an abundance of buttons to press along my bedside, but none related to my new-found symptoms.

I had experienced excessive blood loss, treated with distressing hours of transfusions. While I was trying to withstand the painful transfusions, I cried out to God and pondered life with mixed emotions. I wept in the sadness of never being able to conceive. I had deep feelings of loss and felt empty, like my heart had also been removed. I was a young lady in my late twenties going through the change of life. No one had warned me what to expect because of the urgency of the surgery. It was a traumatic, striking change to process along with the hormonal imbalance issues.

While I was home recovering from the calamitous surgery, the view from my window was of a robin building a nest. I discovered a lesson in fortitude and persistence while observing this expectant mother taking numerous beakfuls of mud and twigs to form a home. Several days later, I was given the rare opportunity to capture video of the baby birds being fed. It was fascinating to be close to the nest and view tiny, open beaks waiting for their meal. The whole time I watched the robins, I pondered different avenues for me to become a mother and build a steadfast home.

During those years of an unknown future, I trusted and believed that somewhere over the rainbow bluebirds and heavenly angels were singing, "Rosie, you will be a mother someday. God will allow your broken heart to be whole."

Another lesson in the journey of life is to realize that God has a better plan: His plan, not ours and in His timing, not ours. The day I held my son for the first time, my heart grew in size. I was no longer broken. My son is the child of my heart. I have always told him that he is the most special child in the world because he grew in my heart for almost eight years: the length of the adoption process.

I believe God didn't allow me natural childbirth in order to make my heart big enough for the birth of adoption to take place.

Each of my son's first-time milestones was treasured and captured with the camera lens. His first smile, bath, coo, giggle, tooth, crawl, step, and word were all embraced with thankfulness. Our lives overflowed with bounteous love. Keepsake photo memory books were compiled in abundance. My life was enriched with happiness and full of promise.

Amen to the miracle of life, however it happens. I have never been as blessed as I am being a mother. He is the joy of my life, and always will be.

One of the greatest gifts God gives us is a child, be it through adoption or natural childbirth. Becoming a mother or father is faith and trust in a higher power. God is the one that is able to manifest that miracle of love and life.

Working full time pulled on my heartstrings. Each morning I had to leave my son was agony. When he was two years old, I decided to make a career change from a job I had enjoyed for twelve years; I started Rosie's Infant Daycare. I felt I had more than enough love to give another child one-on-one devoted attention. This would also allow my son to have a sibling during the day, so to speak. Life was good. I loved being a stay-at-home mother and daycare mommy. I started with a special newborn girl. After this little girl moved to another city, I cared for a three-week-old baby girl. In a few months, her sister arrived into the world. My son enjoyed helping take care of his daycare sisters as he got older. Fostering little people's growth was an important, heart-satisfying job.

Before I knew it, the first day of kindergarten arrived for my son. It was an emotional day for me. Maybe it is for all parents, to know that their child is of school-age. When I picked up my son after that first day of him being at school, he ran and gave me a huge hug. Looking me straight in the eyes, he exclaimed, "Mommy, I missed you so much today, but I remembered that you are always with me in my heart!" My boy: a special love like no other.

My health was becoming more fragile. I thought I would be forced to close my infant daycare business. Then God orchestrated a special request from a loving family in 1996. A young couple expecting their first child called me. I had never met these kind souls before. The parents of the mother-to-be had both passed away, due to a car accident. They were to be the daycare provider for their grandchild. Their tragic story touched my heartstrings. I knew God had made me an instrument to care for this baby, and I would be given enough strength to do so.

When my own precious son was at school, this happy infant's presence gave me the will to keep on with the fight. During months of being ill, I would snuggle him in my arms as his angelic smile beamed hope. My physical pain would subside for a while into those peaceful moments promising a new tomorrow.

This family had enough love in their hearts to invite me to witness and experience the miracle of life with the birth of their youngest children. A different format of motherhood was woven in my heart by sharing in these two amazing births, one natural childbirth and one C-section. Threads of love intertwine me to their family forever.

May of 2012 brought the profound experience of being in the front rows at Mankato State University. I was there to witness my beloved son walk across the stage to receive his degree Bachelor of Science in Biology: Concentration in Zoology. I was thrilled to be alive to see this day. My baby had grown before my eyes and was now a college graduate, a young man on his own making his path in life rewarding. My heart pounded with excitement when his name was called and he reached across to shake the professor's hand to receive his diploma. His childhood flashed through my mind. I lovingly envisioned the first time I held him and a year later, the first time he stretched out his arms, saying, "Momma hugs." I also relived the deafening moment my doctor told me, "Prepare yourself; it is doubtful you will live long enough to see your son finish middle school." Years later, happy tears streamed down my face as he graduated from college. I thanked God for saving my life, allowing me to be alive to share in this special day. My parents, his loving grandparents, certainly must have been watching from heaven above, sharing the pride and honor of his accomplishments. He had succeeded through all of his health issues and my chronic illness, dedicating years of hard work to meet his goals and graduate.

Life had thrown curves in our path, but together we never stopped having the faith to fight the fight, to survive to see this day take place. We had won battles some knew nothing about, and never will. We celebrated after the ceremony with a close group of friends. It was a joyous occasion of life and love, another day of thankfulness, gratitude, love, and blessings.

*******

In the silence of the early morning of March 15, 2008, I awoke with excruciating chest pain. The pain was so severe I sat up in bed to try to breathe. I was sure I was having a heart attack. I collapsed back onto the mattress with a moan. I was in a fog of whiteness and heard fluttering. There was no sense of time, only pureness, and feeling blanketed by soothing peace.

I heard a ringing in the distance. The ringing didn't subside, and finally jolted me out of the haze of tranquility. When I realized it was the phone, I answered and heard the panic in my brother's voice. He asked me to come in haste to our mother's home, about a mile from me. The ringing of a telephone changed the course of the day and set me on my next path in life.

When I arrived, I was stunned to see my beautiful mother dead in her bed. Her hands were still warm; I held them until they turned cold. I gently closed her eyelids. One opened back up. It was meant for me to see the journey she was taking. Within her right eye, I saw crystal brightness, a tunnel of the highest, intense beam of light. I could see through the blueness of her eye the journey of overwhelming peace, light bathing her and taking her soul back to her divine origin. What a gift from God this was, to witness this transition: His blessing of everlasting life for us in the realms of heaven's wonderment.

My mother had been blessed with her final wish to pass in her own bed, in the familiar surroundings that summoned her memories, and to be carried to eternal life with my father, her loving husband whom she had missed every day.

I had brought her home from the heart hospital sixteen hours previously, full of life with a glow upon her cheeks. She had been hospitalized for several days to have thirty pounds of fluid retention drained, buildup due to congestive heart failure. Now she lay pale and lifeless.

My mother had witnessed firsthand my suffering throughout the years, and this gave her much anguish. She had always wished for my adversity in painful tears of endurance to end with a flood of healing. After each of my surgeries, she was by my side as the primary caregiver. She gave me complete consolation, trying to bond my broken pieces back together with her motherly glue.

I am sure you have realized that my sharp chest pain happened when my mother was experiencing her heart attack. I know with all that I am she was trying to take me with her on the journey to heaven. My mother's love was so undeniable and deep for her daughter that she wanted to take me with her to heaven's peace of no pain, but again, it was not my time to leave.

When I rose from the side of her bed, my knees were so weak it was like a rug had been pulled out from underneath my feet. I noticed I was not attached to my feeding apparatus. I do not recall detaching myself before I left home. I will always wonder who detached me from my nutritional therapy. *Did it happen when I was floating with angels earlier that morning?* I wondered. It was a wonderful reassurance to know that someday, I will be free of all those machines.

I heard a train rolling by. The vibrations rattled the dishes in the kitchen cupboards. The train whistle seemed to be echoing. I heard "All aboard... Heaven bound," in my mind.

Hearing the quintessential train sounds, I envisioned my parents as young newlyweds watching a classic steam engine in the late 1940s, chugging along the railroad tracks near their home. I tried to imagine how it would have been during that era. My mother, no doubt, was outside hanging wet laundry on the clothesline, crisp, white sheets floating in the summer breeze while my father used an old-fashioned push mower to cut the front lawn. The sweet scent of fresh-cut grass must have permeated the air. The steam engine's majestic appearance and calming sound in the background would have made for a picturesque keepsake video.

Acute nostalgia from my childhood days of running barefoot through the water sprinkler or playing Annie, Annie Over with my brother, and hearing mother's voice calling us in for supper, encompassed my whole being.

When the funeral home transporters arrived, I was jostled back to reality with my memories put on hold. I was overcome with devastating emotions when they wheeled my mother outside of her home into the waiting hearse. I wept in stunned silence, my heart pierced by each tear. That moment is still frozen in my memory. My brother reached out to hug me, and standing together, we watched them drive away. A cardinal appeared and sang in a nearby tree. I am not sure one ever gets over empty gut feelings of observing a beloved parent's departure. Life on Earth is way too short.

*******

Have you ever had a dream so real you are positive it actually happened, and had to share it with the world? On February 18, 2009, my mother's first birthday in heaven, I felt someone take my hand. I floated with this person, then a hand pointed to a woman's back and the woman turned. It was my beautiful Mother. She was looking at a captivating view. I could also see mountains, a majestic river, lush green grass, flowers of every color, and bright sunshine. She was excited to tell me she no longer needed glasses to view all of the beauty around us. She also told me what I was experiencing was real, and was not one of my photographs. I asked her where my father was, and she stated, "Over there." I again felt like I was floating, and woke up in a daze. I believe my mother hasn't stopped trying to get me to heaven, if only for short visits or glimpses of the wonder, astounding peacefulness, and beauty of our eternal home. There isn't a day that goes by that I don't wish I could dial her former phone number and speak to her, asking for some kind of needed motherly advice.

Her spiritual presence is felt when a butterfly flutters around me. I am filled with peace when this happens, and grateful for her undying love. Recently, before a medical appointment, a lady approached me and exclaimed, "Your mother is looking for you!" My startled response was, "My mother is in heaven." She turned and said, "She is closer than you know." I rejoice when spirit-filled moments happen. To feel angelic love encompass me is restorative assurance.

My mother was an excellent seamstress. She sewed most of my attire, and hers. She was also a master chef in any kitchen, and was head cook at the Litchfield, Minnesota public school system. This was in the era when everything for noon lunch was made from scratch, even the bread. Imagine the tantalizing aroma of homemade bread floating through the school corridors. A wholesome, home-cooked meal is what she prepared for hundreds of children each school day, for twenty-two years. No processed fast food was delivered to be served. She enjoyed seeing each child go through the food line, and loved chatting with them. My husband remembers her giving him an extra banana half on a particular day when he was the last child in the serving line. You recall the little things in life that impacted you with kindness.

I also enjoy cooking and baking for my loved ones. The aromas permeating the air are an emotional comfort to me, as I can't taste the food I prepare. My son asks for Grandma's scalloped potatoes each Christmas. I try my best when making his request to put as much love into preparing them as she did. I feel it is fitting to share her recipe with you.

## Mom's Scalloped Potatoes:

### Ingredients:
6 large russet potatoes, peeled and sliced
3 tablespoons butter
3 tablespoons flour
1 ½ cups half and half
1 cup diced ham or vegetarian crumbles
¼ cup onion

### Preparation:
White sauce: Melt butter over medium heat, stir in flour and cook for one minute. Remove saucepan from heat and whisk in the milk. Return pan to heat, simmer and stir until white sauce is thick. Remove from heat. Combine the diced onion and ham or vegetarian crumbles in a small bowl.

Spread ⅓ of the white sauce in the bottom of your roasting pan. Place sliced potatoes over this mixture. Spread ½ of the ham or vegetarian crumbles with onion over the potatoes. Continue layering potatoes and ham or vegetarian crumbles.

Pour the remaining white sauce over the top layer of ingredients.

Bake covered 45 minutes at 350 degrees until golden brown. Serve warm or let cool, then refrigerate to serve the next day with your meal. Savor the flavor.

# THE APPLE
# OF HIS EYE

The circle of life is complex. In 2001, I became one of the primary care-givers for my father. Parkinson's disease was taking a toll on his body. Dad's bravery knew no bounds. He had struggled for years, with symptoms restricting his life more and more each year. A strong-framed man became immobile and wheelchair dependent.

For the next three years of his life, I summoned the inner strength to take care of my own medical needs and his as well. I did not miss a day of helping tend to his needs, unless I was in the hospital myself. Our bond was so strong that when he tried to speak, I understood what he wanted to say and finished his sentences. I was there for him just like he had been for me since infancy, assisting in bathing, diapering, preparing food, and bringing nourishment to his mouth. His once strong hands shook with tremors too severe to get food to his mouth on his own. I miss those days of caring for him. They were the most rewarding and humbling days of my life. I look at a spoon or fork to this day and wish I was able to feed him. Truth be told, I wish I could also feed myself. I miss savoring the taste of food.

The last six months of his life, we were forced to seek nursing care assistance for him. His symptoms were shattering to all who loved him. His strength in the fight to win against this horrendous disease was admirable.

My father had a tender, caring spirit. I am grateful and blessed to have some of those genes. When I tucked Dad into bed for the night I would give him a kiss. Before I left the room, I would always blow him another kiss. He could catch that kiss with a smile on his face, radiating his love for me. With hands trembling and a lot of determined effort to make his arms move, he always blew a kiss back to me. Those precious memories linger in my heart.

It was a privilege to be by my father's side when he gasped for air and took his last breath, then remove his oxygen mask and kiss him goodbye. Pneumonia won in the end, not the loss of his will to fight the consequences of Parkinson's disease.

Waiting for the hearse to arrive at the nursing home from our hometown gave me the treasured reward of holding his hands for two hours. Feeling his once strong hands go from warm to cold is emotionally indescribable. During those hours, I thought about all of the precious moments we had enjoyed together. I reflected on the time he told me I became the apple of his eye when he held me for the first time. That bond never faded.

I was holding hands that had worked hard, all of his life. I saw the fragments of shrapnel still visible on his body from when he was wounded during World War II in Okinawa. I tried to imagine the terror of being on the front lines in a war zone trench for weeks at a time, and the pain he must have gone through being wounded. I wished I had asked him more questions. I imagined his smile when receiving the Purple Heart in recognition of his bravery and commitment to our country. He was a devoted employee with a strong work ethic for forty years at the Meeker County Memorial Hospital, with the title of chief engineer. I remembered him telling me how he had shoveled coal in the 1940s so patients would have heat. I also examined his hands that once shook from Parkinson's tremors, making him unable to care for himself. I didn't want to let go of his strong hands of love. I didn't know how to say goodbye to my father: the man who made me, raised me, taught me, and loved me with no conditions.

My father raised me to love our country and respect our American flag. Every working morning, he raised the flag outside of the hospital where he dedicated his services. Each night he would lower the flag, waving in the breeze. He made sure no part of the flag touched the ground. I marveled at how he folded the flag with precise, specific motions into the shape of a tri-cornered hat, emblematic of the hats worn by colonial soldiers during the War of Independence. He taught me that in the folding, the red and white stripes were wrapped into the blue, as the light of day vanishes into the darkness of night.

The morning of my father's funeral a majestic sunrise peeked over the horizon while family members and friends gathered around the hospital flagpole. His dear friend wrote and spoke a glorifying tribute during the raising of the flag. He has given me permission to share with you.

## Tribute

"It is only fitting that we gather at this flagpole
To honor a man who gave us his heart and soul.
He took a bullet for us during the second World War
And for him, that was just the beginning of a whole lot more.

A dedicated employee of Meeker County Memorial Hospital for
forty years.
As chief engineer, he was always on call.
But he was more than just an employee; he was a friend to us all.

With volumes of knowledge, gallant, caring, loyal and true
Are some of his attributes, to name just a few.
He was the perfect husband and father
So proud of him were his son and his daughter.

As we stand here with Old Glory
Let us not weep or feel sorry,
For he has reached his final reward.
He is now in Heaven with his Savior and Lord,
So, as we raise this flag towards the sky,
Let us remember his examples of how to live, love, and die."
—Gary Sogge

Dad's funeral service was held at the country church in Forest City, MN, where my parents had been faithful members for over sixty years. I proudly gave his eulogy. After the service, the funeral procession traveled eight miles to the local cemetery. It was a time of reflection. We passed through the countryside where as a teen he had worked as a farm hand, and where he had first met my mother. The journey also meandered by the hospital where he had worked. Proceeding into the cemetery's grand entrance was breathtaking. Viewing the United States flags blowing in the warm breeze gave me shivers. My father was honored with a full military gun salute, and Old Glory presented to my mother.

The next week I hummed an American patriotic song, "My Country, 'Tis of Thee" while placing his flag and volley remnant shells in a keepsake shadow box.

"Let music swell the breeze and from all the trees sweet freedom's song does ring."

My father was and still is my hero. Never once did I hear him complain about his limitations, which some may call disabilities. His inner strength, determination, courage, faith, and resolve to never give up under adversity are qualities I admire to this day. His examples have made me a stronger person in my life struggles.

I am fortunate to have had his undying love, which is still guiding me. My father is now my guardian angel. I always sense his presence. He has appeared to me several times; this usually happens before and after a major surgery. The most meaningful time was a few days after his funeral. At the end of the eulogy spoken at his funeral, I blew him a kiss. What happened a few days afterward is beyond the most amazing experience of my spiritual life. I was fully awake and resting in my bed. A bright light appeared above me; I saw my father's face within a water droplet, lingering in the air for a second until I felt my lips saturated with moisture. He was returning the kiss I had blown to him at his funeral. The divine love of that moment will always caress me. It revealed the promise of the future. God's handiwork reminded me to never question, but to go forth with both my father's and my (Holy) Father's never-ending love guiding me.

Mother and I were draped in peace while decorating the plot of my dear father's headstone on the first Memorial Day after his death. It was enchanting, with the Litchfield Jazz Band playing at Lake Ripley Memorial Park a few yards away. The music floated, lingering in the air. In a nearby swampy section, frogs were croaking in time to the music. Birds were flying overhead and landing in trees, singing along with their chitter-chatter. It was a full choir of the most delightful variety of music. We were standing at the exact spot where my father was acknowledged with a full military gun salute. In my memory, sounds of the firing of those volley shots echoed. I smiled, feeling the warmth of a million loving memories.

A few weeks after my father's funeral, I was outside with my mother and brother. A butterfly danced around us, making its amazing presence known. It landed on the railing of the deck, where it rested for several minutes. We could sense Dad was visiting us in a unique way. The comfort of that moment lives with me each day. I also feel his presence when I hear a cardinal's sweet melody outside my bedroom window.

Several years later, my son was driving home to visit me. I happened to be peering out the window as he was steering my father's former pickup into our driveway. I was enthralled to see a butterfly hovering along the side of his driver's door. The monarch appeared to be guiding my son as he drove, and fluttered all around him as he proceeded to the front door of our home. My son visited with me for a few hours before heading back to the city where he resides. He called me upon his safe return to tell me a monarch butterfly had again appeared along the driver's side of his truck as he turned into his driveway, and had followed him to his front door. He told me he could sense Grandpa.

Many situations should be felt with the heart. What a blessing of peace and mercy to be reassured our angelic loved ones are always with us. Remember to take the time to feel the energy of love.

I am blessed with thankfulness. Life is full of miracles; stop and be observant. Listen in the silence to experience spiritual harmony wrapped around you. Angelic spirits surround us with blessings seen and unseen.

# EMOTIONS

A match lights the wick of a candle. Emotions light all the candles I carry inside myself. The radiant light of Heaven's peaceful wonders that I had witnessed had such intensity that I yearned to return to the place of eternal tranquility. Whenever I closed my eyes, I saw pure whiteness. I couldn't sleep due to malnutrition issues, and this caused more sorrow for me. I had feelings of being in limbo: neither here nor there, tugged by both spheres.

Concerned family and friends wondered how I survived surgery after surgery when being sent home from the hospital unable to take medicine orally for the unrelenting pain. I knew I was carried by God when enduring excruciating levels of misery. I would look into the vast starry moonlit sky on sleepless nights and dream with hopefulness to feel the serenity of heaven encompass every fiber of my soul while I struggled through each minute on earth.

When I viewed bright whiteness in the center of a flower, I was able to relive the experience I had been given of heaven. Every inch of me desired to feel that peacefulness caress and overtake me once again. I decided I wanted to speak to a counselor to deal more effectively with living with pain after experiencing the overwhelming contentment of heaven. I knew God was living in me and working through me.

I made an appointment with a counselor, and a family member wheeled me into the office. I told the cordial woman my story. After listening to my situation, she suggested she would like for me to be able to reach outside of my confined walls to the world around me, with the use of a computer by my bedside.

My son was excited when our first home computer system was installed the autumn of 1998. Within a few days, we received a request on ICQ chat from a British author. A bond of trust formed across the blue skies and oceans in the months to come, and we became pen pals.

I was filled with a new purpose to gingerly move my weak body to the side of the bed where the computer desk was located. Checking to see if an email message had arrived gave me new emotions of wonderment. Someone I had never met cared if I lived or died. His mission was to send us encouraging and uplifting messages, along with his children's theater manuscript and poems. My son would print the email, and I would recline in bed and read it aloud to him. For those sparse moments of indulging in reading, I was transported briefly to a place where I wasn't engulfed in pain. This aided me in trying to forget the agony of my frail health and what was going on around me: that I was no more than eighty pounds, fighting to survive while attached to machines with tubes coming out of my abdomen, the hunger of starvation, the pain of the intravenous needle in my wrist, and being confined indoors.

I found listening to peaceful music also helped, tuning out the constant drone of machines that were keeping me alive. Indulging in new avenues of calming moments was the key to unlocking inner-self renewal for survival. This made me feel less in limbo when outbursts of my heart longed for heaven's peace.

My son had supportive friends who enjoyed spending time at our home after school and on weekends. When I was alone during school hours, I looked forward to the times when our home would be filled with beaming faces and vibrations of laughter surrounding me. Their presence was a gift of human warmth and encouragement that life was worth the struggles. One young girl, in particular, became like a daughter to me, and a sister to my son. Those close ties remain to this day. Recently she became a mother, bonding us even more. I adore when we are able to spend quality time together.

I was infused with enthusiastic emotions by being alive to attend each of my son's high school concerts and theater productions. He discovered singing in the choir, and being in drama class also helped enrich his life. My parents and I would arrive early to locate the best seats at the venue. Being a beaming mother in a front-row seat was exhilarating. I was proud of his acting abilities; he radiated courage and strength on center stage while fighting his own health issues with debilitating ulcerative colitis. From viewing my example of endurance, he found he was able to get on with life even when extremely ill. On more than one occasion we shared the same ER room for intravenous hydration, or antibiotics before a performance. We didn't give up.

For high school drama class, he was cast as Mr. Harry MacAfee in *Bye Bye Birdie*. He also participated in the summer community production of *Annie Get Your Gun*, and played one of the T-Birds in the musical *Grease*. I felt blessed to be able to attend each performance. Along with my mother, we would have never dreamed of missing a single scheduled sold-out performance, even if it meant taking every ounce of energy to get out of bed and be wheeled into the venue. Years later, I had someone tell me that during the standing ovation she still recalled the escalating joy revealed all over my face as I watched my son perform. She was correct. My son on stage gave new purpose to each of our lives. We had overcome adversity; we were fierce warriors.

When my son graduated from high school, we went on a long overdue, well-earned vacation. We picked San Diego, California for our destination. We stayed with close friends who treated us like royalty. It was a wonderful bonding time, filled with healing sunshine and memories we will never forget. It felt like being in paradise to be able to enjoy the beauty of new surroundings together. I was assisted by a California agency for administration of intravenous hydration and nutritional formula supplies. Our friends showed us magnificent points of interest that we would have never seen otherwise. Our spirits were renewed standing at the southern tip of California. Experiencing mighty waves crashing on the cliffs, breathtaking sunsets, and making footprints in the warm sand was exhilarating. Viewing my son's expansive smile when he interacted with dolphins at SeaWorld's Dolphin Interaction Program warmed my soul. He became interested in scuba diving, and achieved his PADI Certification that summer. It was thrilling to be watching from the shore when he received this recognition.

*******

The draining emotions of losing loved ones are enormous, taking tolls of exhaustion on even a healthy person. With the death of my father in 2004 and my mother in 2008, the strain of their departure was epic, on top of my weakened health conditions. I not only lost both of my parents, I lost my support system and caregivers, my family unit, the hands and arms that had always reached out to give daily comfort. Their enriching wisdom was no longer available. Navigating life without them is still difficult, especially when alone and bedridden, recovering from surgeries. They were my best advocates and caregivers.

I found struggling to survive grueling a few days after my mother's funeral. I was experiencing extreme pain along with fibromyalgia fog caused by fatigue, stress, lack of sleep, and poor absorption of my formula nutrition. I soon realized the unrelenting pain was being caused by the G-tube. Doubled over with violent spasms, I was taken to the hospital. X-rays revealed the tubing had released in parts, due to the internal bolster breaking. The sections that had released were lodged inside of me.

I felt my angelic parents' presence guiding skilled hands and health evaluations in the hustle and bustle of the hospital-surgical area. I recall being placed in holding station thirteen before the procedure. A pleasant nurse asked if I minded being in a room that some may have thought unlucky because of the number. I had no qualms with it. I told her my father had been honorably discharged from the United States Army, and was awarded the Purple Heart Medal on Friday the thirteenth. He had always found it to be a lucky day and number. She smiled when hearing that story and proceeded to locate a vein for the IV. I prayed in tranquility while gazing at the number thirteen above the door. I knew it had been planned so I would feel their spiritual presence.

Before being taken into surgery, I reflected upon the calming memory of balloons that were released in my parents' honor. At that ceremony, each person unleashed multicolored balloons. Watching them float away in the wind gave me a feeling of serenity. My parents will never leave the place that matters most: my heart, which overflows with precious memories.

I have found others miss them, too. I was at a grocery store getting ingredients to make a special meal for my son when a lady behind me in the checkout lane glanced at me and exclaimed, "You have your father's smile!" She had worked with my father, and told me how much she missed him. Blinking back prickling tears, I thanked her while my smile radiated gratefulness in her recognizing his special features on my face.

On another occasion, I bumped into one of my mother's acquaintances. She asked, "How is your mother?" I was surprised that she had not heard the news. I smiled and stated, "I am sure she is at peace, and reunited with Dad in heaven."

Recovering that summer, I reflected in reverence upon sunsets at Lake Ripley. The wail of a loon punctuated the fall of the night, while rainbow colors emblazoned the sky with depths of radiance. I would meditate in the garden each morning, and was often blessed with glimpses of cardinals. I was honored when a scarlet male posed long enough for me to focus the camera lens and capture his majestic beauty. When I heard their exquisite melody, flickering thoughts of being held in whispering heartstrings made me glow.

# SNOW-KISSED MEMORIES

Have you ever caught a snowflake dancing through the air with your tongue? If you have never experienced this delight, you are missing out on one of the simplest pleasures of life. I started a tradition the first winter of my young son's life: to embrace the joy of making snowmen, mingled with the pleasing sensation of snowflakes melting on our tongues.

As he grew older, ice skating escapades and rolling snowballs developed into the craftsmanship of deluxe snow forts. My son spent happy hours huddled inside hollowed-out snow, playing he was camping. I always had a thermos of homemade hot cocoa in the fort to help keep him warm. One day while I watched him play, I reflected on snow-kissed memories of a blustery Sunday afternoon in 1993. My young son and pre-teen nieces waited with anticipation for well-groomed draft horses to arrive at our front entrance to take us on a sleigh ride. This was in celebration of my father's 70th birthday, as well as my mother's 65th birthday and her victorious recovery from open heart surgery. A cheerful driver escorted our family aboard the sleigh. We bundled ourselves in the provided wool blankets before our winter excursion began. It was a picturesque adventure throughout the countryside. The warmth of love and laughter wrapped around our family members; nestled together while taking in the beauty of snowy nature. The sounds of clip-clopping hooves and sleigh bells jingling still lingers in my distant memory.

*******

Every time I hear the beautiful hymn "Silent Night," I am transported back in time to the timeless grace and holiness of Christmas Eve worship services at my childhood country church. In this church, I was baptized, confirmed, and married; I also delivered eulogies at both of my parents' funerals there. My mother's side of the family always gathered on Christmas Eve at my grandparents' home to enjoy each other's company. Snow covered roads often made traveling the seven miles from their home to the midnight church service eventful. It would have been spellbinding to have taken a horse-drawn sleigh ride to our quaint church to hear the church bells toll at midnight.

Radiant beams of God's pure love filtered through the beautiful stained-glass window of Christ the Good Shepherd and into my heart on each snowy Christmas Eve. Generations gathered in solemn reverence to worship. The lighting of the Christ candles began with one candle at the front of the church, expanding until the sanctuary was aglow with each person holding a candle that flickered hope, peace, joy, and love. After singing the last verse of *Silent Night*, the organ faded away and we blew out the candles. We departed in joy, wishing each other a blessed Merry Christmas. Traveling back home, I anticipated the festive lights that would be beaming throughout downtown Litchfield. Sparkling lights reflecting against the snow-encased garlands were mesmerizing.

******

A major snowstorm took place in February 2013, when a dear friend was visiting from the state of Washington. Upon his safe arrival, major highways closed down due to inclement weather conditions. We decided to go outside and embrace each ornate snowflake. We became young at heart while making snow angels, enveloped in the reverence of pure, fluffy whiteness.

The majestic thirty-foot evergreen laden with snow was breathtaking. The scent of pine filled the misty air and enhanced the essence of making snow angels. My son and I had planted this evergreen as a tiny seedling, when he was in first grade. I never imagined it would grow to such height or splendor at that time.

We both had just lost our second mother figure, and felt the loss of our loved ones' spirits keenly in the silence of making snow angel silhouettes. Pristine snowflakes cascading upon our exposed faces felt like our guardian angels were supplying us with angelic kisses.

By stopping long enough to drink in the glory of God's gift of grace, we were able to detect heavenly peace embracing us. A moment in time we will never forget, it was a bit of solitude amid a busy world.

*******

Central Minnesota received heavy amounts of snowfall in November of 2014. I was bedridden, recovering from a major surgery. With the use of a walker, I was able to take slow, careful steps from my bed to the bathroom. I peered through a window at the snow-covered earth. The luster of sunbeams on the powdery snow was of magical splendor, mesmerizing as the rays twinkle-danced. With much fortitude, I proceeded to locate the camera. The weight of the camera felt like twenty pounds to my weak arms. Looking through the viewfinder, I was in awe viewing visions of crosses glistening on the silent snow. I was infused with peace. God was giving me signs of His wondrous grandeur and reassurance.

A few weeks later, the north wind was blowing along with temperatures below freezing. I heard car tires crunch across frozen, snowy roads while drivers made their way to destinations beyond my sight. I marveled at multiple layers of frost on the window panes. I analyzed each exquisite formation of white crystals on crab apples hanging from a branch touching one window.

I was given enough strength and energy once again to hold the camera. I concentrated to locate the best angle before pressing the shutter button to capture the elegance of winter splendor. Adding to my delight, several of these digital images were later printed on Sweet Conclusions' greeting cards.

God's handiwork is seen in nature and in my life. He continues to carry me through each of my own intricate daily issues, forgetting no details in creating, molding, and carrying me.

Silence is a gift of empowerment. By allowing the hush of nature to caress me, I have learned how to survive more effectively during the whirlwind of pain levels and changes in my life.

# UNWAVERING

In an unhurried pace, I looked over my shoulder and spotted something brown wavering on a frail branch outside. *Is it a leaf or an animal?* I thought. Wondering if my eyes were fooling me, I grabbed the camera from a nearby table to investigate. The picture window allowed for an unobstructed view. Searching for the exact location, I focused the camera lens. I was able to see the crisp details of a hummingbird sinking its microscopic claws into a leaf stem. Battling intense gusts of rain, this tiny hummer clung fiercely to the tree limb bending beneath it. I watched the branch and bird sway up and down with forceful winds causing disruption like they were a vessel sailing on open waters. The bird's weight seemed to be no more than a few grams. The foliage on the tree wasn't providing much of a protective canopy.

Captivated by the sheer determination of this three-inch bird, I thought of a quote:

"A bird sitting on a tree is never afraid of the branch breaking because her trust is not on the branch but on its own wings."
—Anonymous

I knew God had sharpened my eyesight with the help of a magnifying camera lens to view the divine strength of this bird. He exposes miracles around me each day. This miracle taught me a lesson: to never give up the battle during the storms in my life. Even though I was wavering with the reluctance of going through a procedure that day, I was given reassurance that I would survive with the warmth of His arms cradling me.

Still in awe, I proceeded downstairs and into the car. I needed to travel to a hospital in Minneapolis for a tubal replacement procedure. Maneuvering the car through torrential wind and rain, I sighed in relief when arriving safely.

I thought about the hummingbird's unflinching tenacity on the swaying branch as I grasped the sides of the hard gurney going into the surgical room. I held on for dear life, with unwavering confidence that I would get through this painful procedure. Joy filled my heart for the opportunity to have medical assistance available.

Unwavering with His love, I remembered the lesson of this tiny bird's resolution and gave praises to God. I smiled and gave thanks to the staff for their skilled knowledge. They worked in unison, aiding me with subtle means of tubal nutrition.

Tender words that are spoken and cordial actions are very powerful, and so is hope and believing in yourself.

"Hope is the thing with feathers that perches in the soul and sings the tune without the words and never stops at all."
—Emily Dickinson

Dad rocking his Rosie age 1

Rosie age 5

Mom holding her Rosie age
3 weeks

Rosie age 3

Roller-skating assistance
from my brother

Rosie age 7

Family adventures

Mother-of-the-year 1993–
award and artwork by my son

Natural Bridges State Beach,
Santa Cruz, CA

Mother holding me to a standing position–1998

Hugging Dad–2000

Daily feline affection

Rosie with her Mother, and also her
neighborhood Mom

Pole supporting Rosie for
balance–1999

Rosie ready for Sunday
school–age 4

Barnes & Noble event in 2016–Rosie with British author pen pal

Rosie with Pretty Bird

Rosie's love of high heels
and hanging clothes to air dry

Fresh air–2015

Extra hydration for Rosie

IV's for both mother and son–2004

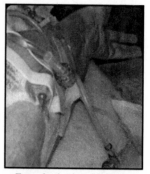

Rosie making snow angels
with her friend visiting from
WA–2013

My mind wandered out beyond the horizon

Rosie embracing life

Roses for Rosie

My heart resonates for my son–
1996

A birthday kiss filled with
thankfulness for my son–2012

My son by my hospital
bedside–2014

Artwork by my son; showing
his mother attached to
machines–1998

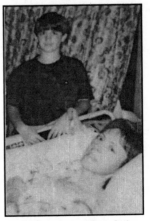

My son by my hospital
bedside–1998

# SOUNDS OF REASSURANCE

Faint rays of sun filtered through the lace curtain. I realized, in the throes of excruciating pain, that it was early morning. After a turbulent night of inadequate sleep, I awoke feeling exhausted, not refreshed. In a short timetable of 21 days, I had gone through three procedures for tubal replacements. I reached with my left hand to make sure the J-tube was still intact on the right side of my abdomen. It was loose, and leaking more fluid than what was being pumped in for consumption. I also touched my left side to make sure that the G-tube was still in place. My robe and bed linens were soaked. I was dehydrated, fatigued, hungry, and feeling faint.

I felt like a flower that had lost all of its petals: incomplete and stripped of all dignity. I was concerned, wondering if I could possibly be absorbing enough nutrition to build the energy I needed to restore those important petals and feel beautiful again.

That refreshing scent that lingers after an April thunderstorm drifted through the open window. I heard the soft, drawn-out sound of a mourning dove. My life had become being in tune with my surroundings while bedridden. I appreciated I had been granted the gift to notice the small treasures in life that often become unnoticed by those who hurry through their day. I was grateful for my senses of smell, sight, and hearing, all mixed with the wonderment of the world beyond my bedroom window. I anticipated the delightful chorus of a cardinal while listening to the coo-OO-oo of the dove.

A stoma on my abdomen had been refusing to hold any size tube. It would spit out the tube with excessive force, resulting in tears and overflowing leakage running down my tummy and spilling onto the bed linens. I was no longer able to get adequate nutrition. In despair, I wondered how I would survive, and what steps were needed for me to get proper hydration and nutrition. I seemed to melt into the wet linens sticky with formula. Being too weary to move, I closed my eyes in meditation.

The day before, I'd had a consultation with a competent surgeon in Minneapolis. After examination, he revealed sections of my intestine had become angry from years of over-usage. All previous procedures had failed in maintaining placement of numerous tubes of different sizes for proper hydration and nourishment.

"Your intestinal area is like raw meat, and will not function any longer," he stated while making direct eye contact. I was not sure I wanted to hear his words. To fathom the realization was devastating news. This was my *only* source of nutrition and survival. I shuddered at the thought. The surgeon continued, "Rosie, I admire your courage. In the nineties, you were a strong woman. Today, I am witnessing an even stronger woman. I would not have been able to endure the pain, hunger, and struggles you have gone through without going insane. This morning you greeted me with a smile. I wonder, do you ever cry?" I replied, "When I pray each night, thanking God for carrying me, yes, I usually cry." There was silence in the room. The surgeon's eyes became moist with tears.

An ileostomy intended to keep a tube in place for a few weeks or months in the 1990s had been working overtime. The surgeon and other doctors were amazed at the miracle of an intestinal section not intended to be used long-term for tubal nourishment to have succeeded sixteen years in sustaining me.

I could understand why it was tired, angry, and had stopped functioning. I had felt all of those feelings way too many times during my daily struggles throughout the years. Sometimes I am only able to endure getting through each moment, one step at a time, instead of dwelling on the whole day to come.

I was very weak and dehydrated. I prayed that trusting acceptance of trials would bring blessings that somehow would outweigh the feelings of desperation and fear. I had to entrust God for *new* means of keeping me nourished. This meant more procedures and testing with comments like, "Your plumbing is beyond complicated."

The sparse minutes of listening to the cooing of the dove had given me some inner peace. I was feeling calmer and less anxious about the uncertainties of the curves in my journey. I have found there is always a form of gratitude in each small step within each winding path.

It quickly became an emergency situation to find a solution to keep me nourished. After returning to the hospital in Minneapolis, I was placed in radiology with capable physicians for placement of a new nutritional setup for me, a *combined* GJ tube: gastric for decompression, and jejunal for feeding.

I was feeling overwhelmed and in total disbelief with the complexity. In a well-equipped procedure room, my eyes were transfixed on a 70-inch screen while the tubing was placed into the small bowel. I was overtaken with emotions. Tears stung my dry eyes and streamed down my rosy cheeks, evidence of my thankfulness. I would now be able to get adequate hydration and absorb formula nourishment.

When they transferred me from the surgery table to the even harder gurney, the whole three feet of curling tubing felt like it was going to release out of the left side of my torso.

Within minutes, I was in a recovery room to rest before being sent on the long car ride home. My whole body was inflamed in distress. Sore muscles were screaming in agony. I marveled at how I had the ability to move with three feet of tubing inside of me.

This was the second replacement of tubing in a few days. After the first placement, the tube came out of my body while I was still in bed. I screamed in excruciating pain upon its release. The tube ejected with such force it felt like it was strangling me. The balloon holding the tubing in place had deflated. My son was home visiting and heard my screams from a different level of our home.

I sobbed in turbulent pain. My son appeared bewildered. I could tell he was wondering how to console me. He was a dear to confirm that he loved me. I was grateful he was home for a short visit, and took comfort in his presence and words. I did, however, feel this complication had taken away our moments of spending quality time together. He assisted me in standing. Tears flooded my feverish cheeks and I felt faint, with nauseating fluid in my throat. Being so dehydrated, the room seemed to be spinning as well. The intensity of my acidic body fluids escaping from my stoma burnt my abdominal skin. Fluids running down my tummy and legs left me feeling helpless, in utter despair.

While praying for forbearance, I heard a cardinal outside my bedroom window. The whistled song I had hoped to hear while awakening days previously now diverted my attention from the increased pain levels. The rich melody reassured me that my guardian angels would provide guidance during the miles to the hospital, where I had to go promptly—*before* my stoma hole closed, so a new tube could be precisely placed.

In times of trauma, I have been blessed to hear the cardinal sing and to be aware of other spiritual signs, all indications letting me realize that I am not alone in my struggles. God gives reassurance, all done in His timing of perfection, not mine. My course of action is to listen more closely to His whispers.

"Be still, and know that I am God" —Psalm 46:10

# WINGS OF LOVE

Summer is starting to show signs of departure along with indicators of autumn's golden arrival. There is crispness in the air, and the days have less sunlight. Multicolored chrysanthemums carpet the winding garden path. The sugar maple trees have hues of electric orange and red. The azure sky blends everything together for a newly painted landscape.

I was enjoying being enveloped in the warmth of sunbeams cascading through the window-panes when I heard the soothing melody that goes with the lyrics, "I'm sitting on top of the world, just rolling along. I'm quitting the blues of the world, just singing a song."

The tune was drifting from a musical lovebird figurine encased in a glass hutch nearby. This figurine had been a cherished keepsake of my parents that represented their 50th marriage anniversary. The few seconds it played was long enough to give me a slight chill. I often shiver when my soul becomes sparked with spiritual sensations.

I walked outside onto the deck. A butterfly fluttered its dainty wings like angels of God around my head with astounding beauty, and stopped to rest on the patio table. My soul came alive, viewing its distinctive array of colors and one-of-a-kind, prominent markings. I had never seen such an exquisite butterfly. It was gratifying to be able to sense the warmth of love in that moment.

Each time a butterfly appears in my vicinity I feel I have been sent a spiritual signal, letting me know that some form of transformation is about to take place in my life. While being ill, my soul has gone on a spiritual journey. I once felt trapped, throughout the years of challenging struggles when my life took sharp turns down undreamed-of paths. Presently, I don't feel trapped. Amid life's storms, I have grown from situations that could have broken me. A metamorphosis has taken place. I have transformed, and learned how to survive. In a sense, I have emerged from a chrysalis as a transformed butterfly. I am enduring while being carried by God, and soaring with new aspirations.

I am not permitted to lift over five pounds, the weight of my pump and apparatus when I am able to wander from my bed. This restriction doesn't mean I don't try to conquer the world. Some days are filled with more physical energy than others, due to chronic fatigue limitations and health situations. I strive for each day to be a good one. I may lack physical energy, but I have an abundance of ambition. I push and challenge myself with a variety of delightful tasks: photography, writing, creating Sweet Conclusions art, twirling a baton, and playing the piano to name a few. Keeping my creative juices flowing helps keep me balanced.

During a moment of having a boost of energy, I decided to slice crimson stalks of rhubarb to make into a custard dessert for a friend. I held and scrutinized one of the heart-shaped leaves. The vibrant veins were very distinct and deep. *What can I make from this leaf?*

Once I had mixed the ingredients and placed it in the oven to bake, I went outside. I placed a perfect rhubarb leaf face-down on a mound of sand and scooped some cement mixture on the leaf. Letting the cement dry for several hours, I then peeled off the leaf. Viewing the fantastic imprint was exciting and much to my delight, a butterfly hovered around me. After the cement cured for a week, I transformed the leaf imprint with a variety of paint colors. The rich shading of colors made the imprinted leaf come to life. The leaf had been born into a work of art: another form of metamorphosis. I have these stunning creations placed inside my home as table centerpieces, and outside to enhance the garden with a flare of charm. My friends and family enjoy having a part of my creative art in their gardens. Each rhubarb mold transforms to be one-of-a-kind...like we are as human beings.

The heavenly spirit is closer than we realize. Renewing, transforming, and refreshing us with new life. A butterfly sighting is waiting somewhere along your journey. Allow the experience to set your heart aflutter.

# GIVE MY LOVE
# TO ROSE

Surgery day had ushered itself in. Another season and moment in time had begun. My son arrived to drive me to Minneapolis early on the morning of October 1, 2014. When we approached the hospital parking lot, I savored the beauty surrounding me before heading toward the main doors. I stopped to inhale. The last fresh air for several days filled my lungs.

Noticing vivid flowers in a planter, I reached out to touch the delicate petals. A mixture of aromatic perfumes refreshed my senses. A beam of faint sunlight was trying to escape from the gray rain clouds overhead. Light rain droplets touched my skin, and I shivered. I reminded myself to take another moment before entering to focus on peace. *Breathe deeply, Rosie. You know what keeps you going while going through overwhelming trials: your faith, gratitude, determination, and courage.*

Once inside the hospital, my son and I located the elevator to the surgical level. I felt unsettling anxiety and a swelling lump in my throat. I prayed in the silence.

The elevator doors opened, and I checked in with the receptionist. I held back tears of mixed emotions. I knew all too well the painful challenges that awaited me after I awoke from surgery. I filled out paperwork at admissions before being assigned a station to be prepped.

My son was in the room with me when the anesthesiologist asked me questions and placed an intravenous line. My surgery was to begin in 45 minutes. I kept reminding myself that God is always near, giving me the strength to handle the trials of the next hours and days ahead.

The surgeon arrived, and the minute I saw his face I knew something was off. Sitting next to my bed, he explained the decision to bring in the top colon surgeon in our Midwest area to do the actual surgery. He would be the one to assist this specialist. This meant my surgery would not take place at 11 AM, but at 5 PM instead. I was overwhelmed with mixed emotions, but I knew God had this under control. A new plan was underway, being blueprinted from prayers by so many for success.

He explained he wanted this highly regarded colon specialist to perform a new procedure, which hopefully would ensure long years of nutrition and life for me. I asked, for reassurance, "Will you be in the surgical room during the procedure?" He looked into my eyes and said, "Rosie, I wouldn't miss this for the world."

Remember, this compassionate surgeon was the man who performed what I call my life-altering surgery in the 1990s. I had confidence in him. I felt tranquil reassurance that his decision to bring in the colon specialist was correct, and led by God's plan. My son reassured me the best had been made available to perform surgery on me, and we should agree to proceed.

I gave my consent and was sent to a private room on the third floor until 4:30 PM. It was a blessing to have my dear son and his caring friend waiting with me. Their calmness brought me serenity. A nurse noticed me shivering in the lightweight gown. She wrapped heated blankets around my quivering frame. I was able to relax, and enjoyed a short siesta while my entourage went for lunch. A thoughtful friend had a gorgeous bouquet of multicolored daisies delivered. The beauty of the flowers adorning the mundane hospital walls zapped the drab room into a soothing flower garden. To assist in lifting my spirits, I closed my eyes and imagined a monarch butterfly alighting on the nearby daisy petal. Flowers in a hospital room are important. They bring the joy of my love for the outdoors inside and help instill hope, which promotes healing.

For the next seventeen days, that hospital room became my home base while enduring unrelenting pain, weakness, nausea, and more challenges when they presented themselves.

As I was being wheeled into surgery, another heated blanket was placed around my shoulders. It was luxurious to feel the warmth cocooning my trembling body in the icy surroundings of the surgical room. To get through the procedure with grace, I told myself the blanket was a reward for my stamina, the heat radiating the warmth of God's love and peace. I prayed for the medical staff and surgeon's hands to be guided.

*******

My experience awakening post-anesthesia is an abstract art piece, a mixture of blurred images, confusion, and feelings of uncertainty all tumbled together in extreme slow motion.

I recall trying to open and focus my eyes for a mere second, on a nurse who was next to the bed. He told me his name. I tried to speak. "Smiling face," skipped across my lips. I felt the sensation of his warm hand on the side of my cold wrist taking my pulse. He answered with a soft voice, "Yes, Rosie; I put a smiling face after my name on the whiteboard before your surgery. It is wonderful you are relating that to me telling you my name."

I closed my half-open eyes, thanking God for holding me through surgery and allowing a compassionate nurse to imbue my surroundings with a simple gesture of kindness. Days later, that same nurse entered my room to tell me he was appreciative I had noticed his smile, and wanted to thank me. Acts of caring, however minute, are important to me. My life has transformed into finding and focusing on a thin needle of hope while enduring a haystack of smothering pain.

I awoke the next morning, and my shoulders were in excruciating pain. My abdominal surgical area was numb from the epidural needle in my spine. I was throwing up pure bile, making the pain level in my shoulders unbearable from the wrenching movements. Pain specialists were brought into my room to examine me. They decided to not move me onto a gurney. Leaving me in the hospital bed, they steered me down long hallways into different elevators, rolling me into a surgical room. They placed a nerve block into my suprascapular nerve endings to numb the pain. This only helped relieve the pain in my shoulders for a few hours. Unfortunately, years later, I still have debilitating pain in my shoulders.

The next day brought more pain and nausea. My son arrived to check on me. I was like a volcano spewing the whole time he was visiting. I remember him saying, "Mom, you are so pale." The warmth of his special presence in the room made me pray harder to continue to withstand this trauma to my body.

Alarms sounding next to the hospital bed seemed endless. Either my oxygen level was too low and alerted me to breathe deeper, or my IV fluid bag was running low and would beep nonstop, or the epidural needle monitoring machine would shriek if I moved wrong in bed.

My body crashed for several hours when my potassium levels dropped, along with no urine output. I saw Jesus' face that afternoon next to my bedside. I felt complete peace. A specialist entered my room and said, "The Holy Spirit is felt in this room."

I often had specialists in my room trying to figure out the complexity of my illness. I had never met two of them. When I asked who they were, they replied, "We heard one hot chick was in room thirty thirty-two, so we decided to check her out," I appreciated them trying to make me laugh while I was in utter misery. I was grateful for the great collaborative team of experts.

It was around 2 AM on October 10th when I glanced at the clock on the wall. I whispered, "Ruthie, happy heavenly birthday." She was a very important lady in my life. A second mother, so to speak, who enriched my life since birth. The monitoring machine attached to me was soon blaring again. When I pressed my call button for assistance, I experienced energy vibrations in close proximity to my bed. Within seconds, a spirit-filled sensation of awareness that someone had sat down on the left side of the bed occurred. I closed my weary eyes; taking in the love I felt surrounding and caressing me.

I heard footsteps and someone entering my room. A quiet voice echoed, "Dear, I need to put on more lights." She gasped at my name on the wall information board and exclaimed, "Your name is Rose!" Appearing as if she was in dismay over my first name, she looked at my wrist ID bracelet. I noticed her misty blue eyes filling. She spoke in a soft voice,

"I am sensing a strong spirit of love in this room, moving me to tears." She went on to explain that when she entered the room, a verse from the Johnny Cash song entitled "Give My Love to Rose" went through her mind. After seeing my name, she knew she was an instrument being used to relay a message from one of my loved ones in heaven. When she left my room, I wept to have had such a blessing of love bestowed upon me. Pure exhaustion padded with a wonderful assurance of being protected gave me a few hours of slumber before the next alarms sounded.

When my eyes fluttered open, I noticed a white sheet of paper on the blanket. I reached for the paper, to read the lyrics to the song "Give My Love to Rose." The nurse was spirit-filled and must have printed the song's lyrics for me to keep. I will never forget that moment. I have kept the printed lyrics as a token of one of my numerous angelic hospital experiences.

I had overbearing discomfort from vagal reflex, causing constant spewing. This escalated my shoulder and abdominal pain levels, also prompting excruciating headaches. Often the room appeared to be spinning out of control due to dehydration issues. I was fortunate to feel God with me every second, helping me endure the struggles, giving me the strength to fight the hopeless, stressful pain levels. His reassuring love always seemed to be caressing me throughout the painful journey of healing.

On day 17 of being hospitalized, the insurance decided it was time for me to be moved out of the hospital. I was given the choice of 100 days in a nursing home, or home care. My body was so frail, yet my mind was strong and optimistic that home care was the answer. I wondered if I was placed in a nursing home setting for that amount of time if I would fall through a trapdoor of depression. At least at home, I would have purring concern and comfort from feline companions. The quietness of home would be a wonderful welcome versus the ceaseless barrage of noise in a hospital or at a nursing home. It has been proven when patients don't sleep because of incessant sounds, they don't heal as quickly. Another added bonus: no one would awaken me from peaceful slumber to check my non-urgent blood pressure.

Once home, the horrendous days of being bedridden stretched into months. I had perceived moments that I was perhaps close to heaven's gates. I was allowed glimpses of heaven during this time. I saw loved one's faces, Jesus, and heard angelic voices singing hymns of praise. I was permeated with peace and felt the life forces of souls surrounding me. I still feel the intimate nearness and energy from loved ones while I continue to fight and win this battle.

To be bedridden 24/7 and stricken with painful weakness heightened powerful, roller-coaster emotions. Never did I feel angry when lifeless, though. I always felt faithful comfort that the best was yet to be. It was déjà vu of the 1990s, with moments of hopelessness and unabated pain. I was ready to experience heaven's wonders.

I was blessed with skilled, kind-hearted physical therapists and occupational therapists assisting me in waking up my weakened body. I struggled while experiencing pain levels off the Richter scale. Relearning how to control breathing when in constant pain is an art. I was given simple bed exercises to help prevent blood clots and bedsores. Trying to move sore muscles made me cry out in pain. Inch by inch, I would slide my frail body to the side of the bed. It was a challenge without throwing up bile and having the tubing attached to me get tugged. It took complete determination to move my legs over the side of the bed into a sitting position, and to find the inner strength to stand. With an aide and a walker for support, I took eight steps from the bed to the bathroom. I would rate that amount of endurance as something like climbing up a steep incline to reach a mountaintop. Saturated in a weak sweat, I had succeeded in getting out of bed—not a simple feat. I had won the jackpot. In recognition of this success, I imagined bells going off and glittery confetti flying everywhere, with a net of balloons opening and floating down from the ceiling. Through the pain, I smiled. There is a connection between weakness and strength. When I wither with weakness, my strength starts to grow.

Weeks after surgery, I was given increased patience not to be overwhelmed. I wasn't strong enough to accomplish the simplest of tasks: washing my own body and hair. The loveliest aid arrived twice a week. She blessed those days in the most understanding ways by wiping my tears while saying, "Rosie, believe me, you are beautiful and determined." With the help of a safety harness and her assistance, I was able to sit on a chair in the shower for a few minutes to have her bathe me. On day 116 of being bedridden, I was able to go from sitting to standing in the shower with assistance. To have penetrating warm water flow on my sore shoulders and down my lower back was too incredible for words. Those few moments of freedom—to feel alive—were electrifying, but also exhausting. After the shower, she would dry my body and hair, apply lotion on my dehydrated skin, and style my hair with unique braids. Bringing a mirror to my bedroom chair, I was able to view my latest hairstyle. I always gave her praises. The rewards of being clean and seeing my different hairstyles were mentally powerful. She used my cellular phone camera to take a photo of each new style. For fun, a photo collage was compiled of the different braided hairstyles. I placed my favorite styles on my Facebook page for friends to view and vote on which one they liked the best. I received many responses, but style number six, of the upside-down French braid with curls on top, won. I found that ironic because my life was an upside-down blend of trying to find normalcy.

Talented, caring aides and specialists entered my home the first day as strangers. Through bonding by stating, "We can do this together," they became trusted friends. Each time they went the extra mile, it made a huge difference in my survival.

Never underestimate the thankfulness of compassionate kindness when going about your daily life. Gifts of caring have revitalized and bolstered my spirit. Spread sincerity mixed with loving phrases around cheerfully. I suggest we clothe ourselves in showing compassion and warm-hearted feelings.

I found living alone difficult after this major surgery. I missed my mother's helpful care and comforting love. I was grateful to be surrounded by the felines next to me. Their purring vibrations gave me moments of tranquility. I know I would have been more despondent without their unconditional companionship. Animals sense so many things that some humans seem to not understand. When I cried out in distress from my pain levels, they knew to comfort me, and did so without hesitation. The youngest cat insisted on kneading my shoulders. Maybe she sensed how blocked my shoulders were by pain. She also insisted I hold her dainty white paw after she had gently wiped my tears of sorrowful pain, which had streamed down my flushed cheeks. I sometimes felt she was an angel, not a cat by my side caressing me with healing comfort.

Droplets of hope whispered serenity within my soul on day 166 of being bedridden. I was awakened by the crystal clear, reverberating sound of my dear mother's voice, saying my name: "Rose Ann." I was filled with thanksgiving upon hearing her voice after eight years. My eyes grew wide with wonder when I caught a glimpse of her beautiful face. She turned, revealing a back view of a white flowing gown. She ascended as if walking up steps, with a foggy, pure whiteness surrounding her. She soon vanished from my sight. At that exact moment, I was gifted with a flash of my father's face; he was smiling. I was surrounded with complete, loving calmness. Deep vibrations penetrated throughout my whole body. He vanished as quickly as my mother had. I did not feel sadness in either of their departures. I found solace in those moments.

Four hours later, I unveiled the miraculous story to my home care nurse, when she arrived to change my bandage and clean my wound site. To our amazement, the deep hole at the end of my abdominal incision was closed when the nurse uncovered that area. The awestruck look on her face and mine must have been priceless. I imagined the joy of my guardian angels viewing our discovery. The day before, I had a visible tunneling hole at the bottom of my incision; a photograph had been taken to show that after five months, it still was not healing. I had an upcoming appointment to see the surgeon for further evaluation.

There was no doubt in my mind or the nurse's that the experience of vibrating, heavenly energy closed the incision site. The nurse took another photo of the closed and healed wound. Examining both images revealed an amazing transformation. I still get goosebumps, realizing day 166 was the exact date my mother went to heaven eight years prior. I have learned the magnitude of the possible: the miraculous power of heavenly love.

Love is a wonderful emotion; it brings us together, wherever we may be. When I inhale love and exhale gratitude, I am able to embrace challenges in reaching goals I never thought I would be able to attain, surviving and thriving against all odds.

God's love ties us together and helps us carry the burdens of life with a lighter load. Give someone special in your life an extra dose of love; it will fill them with a warmth that will make them shine with new inspiration.

# ACCEPTANCE

I glanced into a mirror and said aloud to my reflection, "Delicate Rosie, you haven't eaten real food *orally* in twenty years. Weaklings can't pull that off. You have defied the odds and are alive after undergoing another complex surgery. You are an original masterpiece."

I had a flashback of my father, expressing in a humorous manner, "You really know how to do things up right." Viewing all of the tubing attached to me, I had to agree his remark from years ago was still valid. I smiled with the warmth of his heavenly love caressing me.

Smiling mixed with laughter is without a doubt the best medicine. Believe me, this is not always an easy task. Some moments I have failed, not being able to laugh. I have cried countless tears while taking care of my wounds. Low nutritional levels and autoimmune deficiencies have many side effects. Dealing with those adverse reactions are avenues in my life's chemistry that often make me feel out of sorts. Being blessed to be able to belly laugh with a friend gives me renewal in the gift of fighting this battle.

Throughout the years, it has never gotten any easier when I leave my home and proceed to the sea of public eyes. The survival apparatus attached to me is often studied in bewilderment. I try to understand their curiosity. Shopping with my son or going through security at an airport terminal, I have had insensitive adults make cutting remarks. Thoughtless comments stab like a knife into my heart. I need to remember that their cruel words do not define my worth. They were made because my outward persona didn't match what they felt was the norm. The depth of my soul is immeasurable by my outward appearance.

It is a shame when we miss beauty because we are too critical, seeing only the imperfections in a piece of fine pottery. Instead, it would be better to view the intricacy of what God molded in clay. I have worked hard to shine in making myself whole through adversity. The fine scars from surgery and visible components of tubing assist in making me whole and are vital parts of my molding. God made us all distinctive masterpieces.

I have noticed children see me in a different light. They seldom question my way of being fed. If they do ask innocent questions, I answer them in the simplest of terms. They look at my smile and envelop me with their warm energy. I feel blessed when I am fortunate enough to spend time with a child. Their enthusiasm and lightheartedness are pure joy. If you go searching for a special pebble, it becomes a glorious treasure to hold in your hand for hours. There is always time to stop and investigate a bug or smell a flower's sweet perfume. Their world is full of adventure and awe. Pure innocence abounds with loving force, and sharing precious moments together fills my soul to capacity. Spending time baking with children is pure merriment, punctuated by giggles. I find delight in watching their expressions when they take their first nibble.

Life's difficult lessons often seem to be smothering, especially when bed-ridden. Several years ago, my mother asked me, "Are you going to allow these hardships and trials to harden your heart?" She then left me alone in the hospital room to ponder her valid point. An aide arrived with a food tray a while later. After reading on the patient whiteboard my restriction of no in-take orally, she knew she had entered the wrong room. When she turned to scurry out of the room, I noticed a mouth-watering popover on the tray she was holding. Being hungry, I hoped the patient receiving that nourishment would feel well enough to savor each bite.

Have you ever noticed how popovers rise high over the pan with a golden crust, yet when you break them apart, they are hollow inside? This is similar to how I was feeling. I had tried hard to raise my head high, but I felt lifeless and hollow inside: like a cold, torn-apart popover. I could not even cry. I felt too deflated from the extreme pain, causing despair. In my desperation, I wanted someone to hold me and tell me everything was going to be okay. My heart needed interaction and mending.

I prayed for my body to heal with renewed love and to find the strength to withstand the pain of life gone wrong. God was already carrying me; I knew He wanted me to find peace and allow my heart to be light and carefree, like a child's love. I needed to lose the bondage from my past and present painful experiences. The pain I was feeling needed to diffuse and be set free. I could not allow my mind to overmix my sad sentiments. Those emotions needed to pop over the top with love's buttery warmth.

The only way for me to mend my heart is by loving myself and others more. Yes, even when my heart feels wounded, lonely, and bitter with emptiness. My mother was correct. I never wish to close off pieces of my heart so that one day no one will be able to get inside, because it has hardened and become hollow. By loving more, my heart pours forth additional love and grows deeper in the reassurance of who I am: a sensitive, caring, charismatic, unique, and loving woman, mother, and friend.

God has formed and created each of us for a reason, purpose, and plan. Through hope and faith, I believe sadness will evaporate. With every fiber of my being moving forward with acceptance, my smile doesn't ever have to be forced. It will continue to radiate God's love within me.

This is why I share my story with you now and through motivational speaking. By reaching out and sharing, my sensitive heart meets another heart that needs strength to face their own battles. God is the one that gives me a glow that radiates deep from within, showing others I am carried.

Recently, at a Sweet Conclusions event, people in the audience were wiping tears after hearing me speak. My story touched their hearts. I have found that writing about and sharing my experiences, and expressing my feelings, has helped strengthen a multitude of deep emotions. Some of those emotions had been locked away for years.

I have written this whole memoir while bedridden at various points in my life. God has given me words in the middle of the night to express my inner thoughts. After innumerable surgeries and extreme weakness, I may be at one of my lowest points in life, but I'm not giving up on hope and faith. Tomorrow is a new day. I have lovingly planned for each new step I take into the future.

When you journey through your daily life, search for heart-shaped items. You will find them displayed in several different locations, textures, colors, and forms. I marvel at what I have found revealed in heart-shapes: rocks, clouds in the azure sky, fragrant flowers, bark on a tree trunk, delicate heart-shaped markings on a butterfly's wings, or in a bird's feathers.

The spring my mother passed away, I stumbled upon her bleeding heart bush. Not one but two perfect hearts in full radiance were dangling from lacy foliage. They welcomed me, and were intertwined just like my parents' hearts in heaven must be. The heart-shaped blossoms were just waiting for me to discover them. I viewed them as another sign that life goes on eternally. What a blessing of grace and hope, to be reassured their love is always with me! I enjoyed capturing those intertwined hearts with the camera lens. I had the image enlarged, matted, and framed for a wall in my home. It was also printed on a Sweet Conclusions greeting card.

Many moments are plainly felt with visual signs and spiritual energy surrounding us. These experiences are priceless.

Enjoying a car ride in the vast countryside, I noticed a large cloud in the form of a heart. It appeared to have an angelic form in the darker shading. This revealed that love surrounds us every minute of our life. God paints volumes of love all around us. I need to remember this during moments of difficulty.

Dealing hour to hour with tubal issues is a challenge. The connector attached to my tube that allows nutrition to enter my body detached one morning. I awoke to saturated bed sheets, and my body covered in the sticky formula. When this happens, my debilitated body suffers even more, due to lack of hydration. Dehydrated, I was shaking and dizzy while attempting to shed my wet clothing and change into dry attire. I finally succeeded, and slipped on a robe.

I had gone outside for fresh air to help clear my frustrations when I felt wetness dripping down my tummy and legs. Again, the connector tubing had unhooked. The formula was now running all over the cement patio. I was in total weak despair, and the tears started flowing. The overwhelming exasperation of trying to get hydration and nutrition into my body had failed once more. I gasped when I noticed the leakage had made a heart-shaped puddle on the cement patio. It was humbling to see what appeared to be the shape of a Band-Aid inside the exact center of the sticky, moist heart-shape. I knew not to give up; a sign was being given to me verifying that my body and spirit were not broken or hollow beyond repair, but were being mended. I was being told that I *would* find a way to endure, and this also would pass.

I exclaimed praises, "You are all around me. I feel your love carrying me and showing me signs not to give up when frustration happens. Thank you for allowing my heart to be open to view this amazing sign. I can and *will* succeed."

Through the timing of signs, I have learned beneficial lessons in keeping the faith and how to cope with adversity. Each adversity has made my heart more sensitive, increasing my ability to feel more deeply. Both are positives. I stop and take notice of life all around me in diverse ways making me grateful for each new moment to be alive. I share my journey in the hope you will understand signs are given to prove we are all carried and always loved, even when we feel alone and scared.

He is always infusing us with His grace. Our hearts are etched with His love. If one person doesn't know God's love, and I am able to touch that person, then His purpose for me writing about my journey in this memoir has been achieved.

My sign from above: This is formula draining from my disconnected tube, making a heart-shape with what looks like a Band-Aid in the center. This semblance of a Band-Aid was a small section of the 4x4 piece of gauze that had been covering my stoma. Due to the moisture, a piece released and fell to the ground, making this experience even more divine.

# FOUR–LEGGED
# NURSES

Many people don't give animals enough credit for how in tune and loyal they are to their human families. I call my short-haired critters my four-legged feline nurses. There is nothing like coming home from the hospital to my furry loved ones and hearing them meow. If my quality of life is based on feline hugs and wet kisses, I am blessed.

These engaging feline nurses are most protective when a new healthcare assistant arrives at *their* home to care for me. Truly, they allow *me* to live with *them*. The nursing assistant's every move is monitored under intense scrutiny. Complete inspection of all belongings is conducted, and all scents are examined by wet noses sniffing for evidence. You either get a meow of approval or a growl of disapproval. For example, when a blood pressure cuff is taken out of a nurse's medical bag, it has to pass feline inspection first before being used. They waste no time being in the human nurse's face, glaring to make sure that their mommy Rosie isn't going to be hurt.

My four-legged nurses are vigilant and intuitive in sensing my pain levels.

They stay right next to my side, providing compassionate snuggles and undivided purring attention. They take their dainty paws and rhythmically knead on throbbing sections of my body. It is as if they possess a sixth sense, knowing that their gentle massaging will reduce my pain levels, relieving anxiety. These cats look into my soul. They seem to say with their meows, *"We see through your smile and know you are not okay; we care."* It would behoove us as humans to master this skill to perfection.

One of my kittens is usually on guard at the foot of the bed; if my pump starts blaring, she leaps to alert me by pulling my hair strands gently with her mouth. I feel she knows the pump alarm means danger, that the malfunction is not allowing formula nutrition to enter my body. The youngest cat is my shadow. She prefers to nestle her head under my chin. When tears trickle down my rosy cheeks, she catches the moisture with her small white paws. She insists on falling asleep by placing her dainty paw in my hand, and staring with endearment into my eyes as we fall asleep. This has become a nightly ritual.

All of their compassion is a true gift of unconditional comfort when I am so ill, lying lifeless and only aspiring to survive. In the silence, hearing a purr is a reassuring testament of angelic feline endearment, a distinctive correlation between longer longevity and serenity.

Embracing their freely given heartwarming affection gives me added strength. Engaging in relaxation, I am able to drift off into a peaceful slumber, receiving more reserve to face challenges with lighter steps and a joyful heart.

*******

In the silence, a tender heart stopped beating. For thirteen years, this beloved feline taught unconditional loyalty and compassion to people who entered my home.

It was an honor to hold both of my parents' hands when they passed to eternity. It was an equal honor to hold this companion's paw when she cried out with her last meow. Each experience taught me valuable lessons on cherishing loved ones and life.

Rest in peace, little princess. Thank you for showing me that love can manifest with purrs in myriad ways.

# TEACH ME TO SPEAK
# FROM MY HEART

A full moon streaming through the blinds of a hospital window gave a glimmer of light and hope during the middle of the night. There was endless, noisy disturbance reverberating from the hallway and adjoining accommodations. *Shouldn't everyone be sound asleep at this time of the morning?*

In a 24-hour timetable, the intravenous line had infiltrated three times. The IV site was in excruciating pain, swollen and tender with discoloration and leaking blood. I was feeling like a pincushion, with my fragile veins. An IV team member was alerted to bring a near-infrared light scanner to my bedside to help locate a suitable vein. I was relieved to hear such a machine existed.

A middle-aged technician arrived at 3:30 AM. Her first attempt to locate a vein painfully failed when the vein just didn't want to cooperate in being used. Being dehydrated didn't help the situation. I was in anguish, and the IV tech appeared to be exasperated as she attempted to find a new vein. In a hushed voice, I said aloud, "Dear Lord, guidance is appreciated. Thank you for bestowing upon us your peaceful presence."

The technician seemed calmer. This time the blood return was a success, with the intravenous line in proper placement.

While assembling all of the equipment back onto a cart, the tech blurted out, "Could you please teach me how to pray? I am ashamed of many things I have done in my life. Is it too late for me to learn how to pray for forgiveness?"

When she glanced away from my caring eyes, I knew it had been difficult for her to express her question. I placed my hand on her arm and said, "I am glad you feel comfortable in speaking to me. Please don't feel embarrassed. God loves us. Just say what is in your heart to Him. That is how I pray." Our conversation was interrupted when her pager sounded.

A smile sketched the corner of her lips when she asked, "May I stop by when I am off duty to talk? I feel God's love flowing through you and in this room." I replied in haste, "Of course, I will look forward to visiting with you."

Before I closed my weary eyes, I thought, *No matter what challenges you, Rosie, remain strong; you never know who you may inspire.*

Two days later, she arrived to sit by my bedside. We had a meaningful chat about life. Some say God works in mysterious ways. I have found this to be very true, and at times astounding.

# WHISTLING SOUNDS
# OF ADMIRATION

I don't know any woman that doesn't like to be caught off guard and
showered with affection. We were in a pet store when a yellow-feathered
cockatiel with bright orange cheeks caught our attention with a two-toned,
"Woohoo!" wolf whistle.

Being the only bird in the pet store that interacted with us, we chose
him for my son to have as a pet. The date was on the 11th anniversary of us
becoming a family. I was in great hopes this bird would become a treasure
for him to care for, and would give him companionship.

We discovered several weeks later that cockatiels usually bond with one
family member. Unfortunately, it wasn't my son this captivating bird decided would be his companion. He picked the green-eyed lady of the household, and author of this memoir, instead.

He imitates the song "Pop Goes the Weasel" and repeats "pretty bird" if
in a willing mood. When someone sneezes, he enjoys mocking the sound; he

says, "Achoo!" which in turn makes everyone in the household laugh. He is a smart bird to know that laughter is the best medicine.

He enjoys sitting on my shoulder while I venture around the house doing daily tasks. When in his cage, he insists by chattering to be able to see me. Once he has clear sight of his adored woman, he is silent and happy. He doesn't allow just anyone to take him out of his cage to hold and pet him. Sitting on my finger, he bows his tiny head, begging to have his neck feathers gently stroked. He finds being showered with attention delightful, a true sign of feeling content and safe in his surroundings. What a loyal affirmation of pet bonding!

When I am hospitalized for long periods of time, this sends our lovely bird into complete distress. He stops eating and singing while I am gone. When I arrive back home, his cage is placed by my bedside. He remains as lifeless as I am during the long recovery. He even refuses to be taken out of his cage to fly around the room for his daily exercise. I believe this has to do with viewing me being completely bedridden and still, making him forlorn.

The day I was blessed to make it from my bed to the living room, with the use of a walker and a physical therapist by my side, he then decided to fly. This regal bird flew to show how overjoyed he was that his human mate was alive and out of bed for a few minutes. Animals are so in tune. What a thrilling moment of surviving the odds, just to view him taking flight. The four-legged nurses also watched in amazement. The felines have never attempted to chase after the bird; they know he is part of this family. Animals are such agreeable friends. I have noticed how his feathers have changed colors over the years. He is now a mature, gray-feathered bird with orange cheeks, at nineteen years old.

God blessed me with these little critters to care for, expanding my family. In return they protect and safeguard me, freely giving their undivided attention and affection. We live together in harmony.

*******

I picked a location dear to my heart to watch the 1944 Milwaukee steam engine train go through my hometown in Minnesota. The train was on a roundtrip excursion from Minneapolis. My parents had watched this same locomotive go by daily in the 1940s and early 1950s. They often told me about its charisma. When I viewed this once retired, now restored classic train rolling over the tracks and heard its endearing steam whistle, I was enamored with vibrations of nostalgic love. For me, this was another form of whistling admiration. Yes, completely different than my bird's whistle, but certainly worthy of recognition.

I hope you get the chance to experience the allure of whistling sounds of admiration in your life soon.

# SWEET
# CONCLUSIONS

In a quiet manner, God blesses our daily lives with calendar seasons that unveil striking beauty. Each season graces my existence. The second I look through the viewfinder of a camera, passionate appreciation is born. Positioning the precise angle of the camera to capture a loved one or elements in nature is a work of art I take seriously, being a photographer. Observing the essence of the world around me, I click the shutter button and shine with contentment. Colorful woven visions become a treasured keepsake photograph for me to construct into a lasting memory, as a greeting card or wall art. Photographs are plentiful in my home. I relish the opportunity to relive the moment, again and again.

Several years ago, I envisioned my scenic nature photographs being intertwined with poetic verses my pen pal had written and sent to me in the late 1990s. I compiled this passion the spring of 2011 into unique greeting cards along with a keepsake coffee table book, entitled *Reflections Upon the Waters of Life*. The photo cover reveals a butterfly drinking nectar from a coneflower.

We only have to slow down our pace to observe and be enchanted with the wonderment and detailed beauty of this world. My photography and his poems enhance each other, inviting you to sit back and peacefully slide away from reality on the wings of photo and verse. We have named our cherished creations Sweet Conclusions.

I was humming to the song "Blue Skies" while driving on the freeway to the Minneapolis-Saint Paul International Airport on June 23, 2011. An azure sky sported numerous puffy white clouds. The day I had imagined for thirteen years had arrived, and I was full of anticipation to meet my pen pal for the first time.

Arriving at the airport in ample time, I located an unoccupied bench in the customs area to wait for flight # F1657 to arrive from Europe. For 45 minutes, I sat there and enjoyed people watching. I pondered where travel destinations would take the hundreds of people hustling about the crowded airport. An older gentleman was reading a newspaper close by; glancing at him, I was reminded of my father. I imagined this man was waiting for his daughter to arrive, that she would hurry to embrace his fragile frame. I smiled through the tears pooling in my eyes. My heart longed for the opportunity to receive just one more hug from my own beloved father. My misty viewpoint next caught a baby girl's smiling face. Absorbed by her gracious innocence, I found myself more at ease waiting for custom gates to open.

Watching a security guard unlock a set of side entrance doors, I approached him and made small talk. He told me the plane from Europe had landed. It would be another thirty minutes, and then the gates would open. I asked him to please let a man with a British accent go through customs first. He winked at me and said, "I'll see what I can do." We laughed and he disappeared through the secured doors.

The next half-hour seemed like an eternity. I went to the ladies' room to retouch my makeup and hair to perfection. At that moment, my reflection revealed an attractive woman ready to take on the world. My eyes didn't appear dull and lifeless like they had for years previously; instead, they had a radiant emerald shine. I didn't feel like an empty vessel. I had survived despite the odds to still be alive for our joyous collaboration to finally meet each other.

When the gates opened, a warm rush of excitement energized my whole being. I saw a distinguished man at the far end of the line. I was positive it was my pen pal. It didn't appear he could see me. I noticed he was wearing a navy button-down shirt. He certainly wasn't a figment of my imagination any longer. A security guard noticed my beaming smile and exclaimed, "Must be someone very special that you see coming through security."

"Yes, it's someone I have wished to meet for several years," I replied. How could I possibly explain my deep-rooted emotions to her? I had gone through countless surgeries and physical therapy rehab sessions to be able to stand at these gates waiting for this moment. I had listened to him telling me to hang on for thirteen years, that he would arrive someday to reach his American dream: to see me in person. Now the time had arrived, and he would soon be going through customs' gates to meet me for the very first time. Continuing to radiate inner happiness, I tried to curb the urge to dart through secured doors.

When the first person walked through the customs threshold, my heart was pumping so hard I thought it was going to burst through my chest. The gates closed and opened several more times. I started counting people. I was losing track, and still no dashing British man. The customs gates closed. Several passengers had now found their loved ones and were leaving the airport. They all seemed happy, most with their arms wrapped around each other.

Adrenaline pumped through my veins when the gates opened again—and there he was, standing in front of me. It was surreal to see each other in person. It was an unforgettable interlude strolling to the car.

From morning to night, the days were filled with laughter, fun adventures, author events, and radio and newspaper interviews. My son was our chauffeur as we traveled to the Badlands in South Dakota to view Mount Rushmore and Crazy Horse. We also ventured on a road trip to view Lake Superior in Duluth, Minnesota and crossed into Wisconsin.

It was beyond refreshing to be traveling and not be in a hospital bed or at home bedridden. We had limited time to accomplish all the stops of our whirlwind itinerary. The moments lifted my spirits like I was floating on air. The accurate headlines in the *West Central Tribune* newspaper read:

## Oceans Apart, Longtime Pen Pals
## Bridge Distance to Meet for First Time

We had bridged the distance to finally meet. The photograph printed with the newspaper article was of us by the lift bridge in Duluth, MN. When the time arrived for him to go back to Europe, I would have enjoyed being by his side, going through security to fly to his world. My health wasn't stable enough to travel the distance to another country, however. Instead, I watched him wave goodbye from secured gates. I had met my goal to survive my health issues, and eventually to meet my pen pal.

Pursuing dreams helps keep me believing in my purpose on earth. Envisioning and designing illustrations and layout for my pen pal's first children's book, *A Lesson in the Jungle*, published in March of 2016, was very rewarding. This book teaches a valuable lesson about preserving life within the animal kingdom. This is the same children's theater production story he had shared with me in the 1990s, when I was struggling to maintain myself. Treasured moments often happen at the end of the day, when you take the time to read to your child or grandchildren. Fulfillment happens when they are old enough to read aloud to you. Being featured together at Barnes & Noble and other venues for book signing events is gratifying. We have gone full circle with this dream of a published book.

The journey of Sweet Conclusions' art was created to show that God has a hand in each of our daily steps. My goal is for you to also discover a positive outlook when dealing with life's struggles through our inspiring products. I hope to see you in the audience at one of the life-changing speaking events. We have been given the opportunity to write a blog for Forum Newspapers. Follow along with us at sweetconclusions.areavoices.com.

How appropriate it is, after all of these years of struggling, to have discovered the realization that this journey is all about the sweetness of the conclusion in my life.

# CREATION BECKONS

A haven of paradise is discovered by meandering along any garden path. I love how God has no rules in using color. The vast palette in His coloring box becomes scattered and mingled to perfection among each bud, blade of grass, sunrise, and sunset.

While examining rich assortments of blossoms, I marveled at how the impressive crabapple blooms seemed to be dripping from the branches. A vibrant goldfinch swayed in the breeze with repeated twitters and warbles. Intoxicating floral perfume from roses evoked loving childhood memories.

I heard a phrase echoing from the radio, "I just want to celebrate another day of living, another day of life," when a swarm of dragonflies appeared. They were hovering all around me. I decided to embrace my surroundings and twirled with their sense of power and poise. Each twirl released stressful struggles and harsh challenges that had been bottled up deep inside of me. Being carefree was exhilarating. The velvet sensation of lush grass between my toes was also pleasurable. I discovered during my time dancing that I started cherishing my own existence. It was gratifying to focus on living in the moment.

In the western horizon, I noticed an unusual cloud formation. I was mesmerized, noticing the shape formed a puffy angel wing. It made me stop and contemplate how amazing life is. The camera was nearby; snapping a photo, I kept reflecting upon the peace caressing me.

When I encounter life's joys or struggles, I need not search for Him; He is always there, enriching my life and giving me signs that angels protect and care for me wherever I go.

For the majority of my life, an inner voice of determination has made me fight to get out of bed and reach for the unknown. At times, my mind still wants to entangle itself in distant concerns in the middle of a sleepless night. *Do I need to know what is at the top of the winding staircase in order to take that first step?* I have found that committing to any forward motion is what counts. In reframing my mindset not to worry, I focus upon the horizon, letting my faith be the radar that sees me through the fog.

I would not be a mother today if I had not pursued my dreams and had faith. If I had not fertilized my mind with positive and inspirational wonders, I would not have been standing to view cloud formations and twirling with dragonflies. I would have still been bedridden.

Many objects glisten in the sunlight. I also twinkle with more vibrancy and strength when rays of sunshine penetrate my skin. Yet in the cold darkness of suffering, when no sunlight prevails, I have found that my body quivers and throbs with intense pain. It is in those moments that my true beauty is only allowed to illuminate if there is a light found deep within me.

Chase your own dreams. Find your sunshine. God is right there, taking your hand and helping you with the first step. His reflection is shimmering upon you along the waters of life.

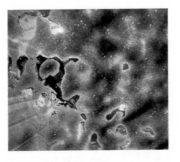

# REACHING FOR
# THE TREASURE

I awoke with a queasy sensation. My eyes fluttered open to a whirling blackness, unlike anything I had ever experienced. The aggressive spinning seemed never-ending. I screamed with a miserable perception of flying off the bed into space. I started spewing. The spinning was not seizing; I gripped onto my pillow for a means of support.

My cat was next to me, crying out in a startled meow. I could hear her amidst the vicious upside-down distortions. I reached out in the darkness for the phone, and was relieved when my shaky hand grasped the receiver. I hit what I hoped to be the redial button. The last person I had called lived a block away. Success was achieved when my dear friend answered. She was able to tell by my urgent tone that she needed to arrive with haste. She decided to call 911.

The ambulance service arrived within minutes. I was dizzy, vomiting, and felt dehydrated with no idea what else was wrong. I was quickly taken out of my home and placed inside the ambulance. My home is in close proximity to the local hospital, but the turbulent ride made it seem like miles.

Throughout the years, I have heard the phrase, "Sometimes you need to look at life from a different perspective." I was frightened by experiencing my world from this distorted perspective. I prayed for my guardian angels to show me a sign of their closeness.

I was diagnosed with dehydration and vertigo: the sensation that either you or your surroundings are spinning when they are not.

Vertigo symptoms have been beyond challenging. I need several pillows when I lie down, to support my head so the room doesn't spin. I can't turn on my side to sleep. I am not able to look straight down or straight up without dizziness and feeling like I am going to faint and fall. Often, I cannot function with the ease of balance that is needed.

In September of 2016, I fell near a stairway due to lingering months of vertigo issues. I felt paralyzed, being alone in my home with no phone nearby to summon for help. I was in pain and too unsteady from the spinning sensation to do anything but remain lying on the floor.

Waiting for the dizziness and spewing to subside, I channeled my functioning mind, trying to drift to a happier time. I allowed the gates of memories to flood open to a time when a beautiful three-year-old girl would arrive at my home and bound up the same stairs I was now lying near. She would leap to the top of the kitchen counter to take off the cookie jar lid. Reaching inside for a sweet treasure, she was aglow with euphoria when she popped a succulent cookie into her dainty mouth. Her blue eyes sparkled with wonderment. She knew that Rosie would always have the cookie jar stocked full. She set about her task with diligence, climbing stairs, and a countertop to reach her treasured goal. She was always triumphant.

I hope she realizes now as an adult that I was giving her a treasure far more precious than different varieties of cookies. I was supplying faithful reassurance that when she reached for an edible delight, the jar would not be empty.

Still unable to maintain a standing position, I pondered life with powerful emotions. I thought of all the treasures I try to reach for in a single day. Sometimes they are not as easily obtained as taking a lid off a cookie jar and reaching inside. Often, what I strive to attain seems endlessly distant, with empty results. How wonderful it would be to grasp for someone's hand to help me, to keep me from falling further down the steep incline! If only someone was right by my side to assist in lifting my body up off of the floor.

Perhaps falling is what was needed to happen for me to remember to pray for more signs that my treasures are also attainable: faithful reassurance that I am not alone in this mixed-up, yet wonderful world. God helps me handle what I have been given, and gives me patience during affliction and the strength to forge ahead like a soldier.

Reaching 2017 marked twenty years of my medical journey of not eating orally. When my phone rings and I hear my son say, "Hello, Mom," I know why I am still enduring.

Seasons have changed: autumn, winter, spring, summer. I have changed. Holidays have changed: Thanksgiving, Christmas, Easter, 4th of July.

Lighting has changed. I have changed. Surgical room lights, glimpses of the bright lights of heaven, sunbeams, more surgical room lights, more sunbeams.

Strength to weakness to strength to weakness has changed. I have changed. Finding inner strength to smile through tears of pain, raising my head from the pillow, to breathe, sit up, stand, to try to balance and walk.

Life is about the dash in between our date of birth and our date of death. There are hidden treasures inside every painful struggle. I seek to continue to search for each of those treasured blessings and grains of opportunity. I never let a day slip away without gratefulness. I try to make each day a new masterpiece.

# FORTITUDE

Social interactions often involve food and liquid refreshment. Dinner parties, picnics, wedding receptions, birthdays, graduations, and anniversary celebrations are centered on what we will prepare for the main course, sides, and dessert, and the beverages we will serve. New Year's Eve customs have us toast in the New Year. Life is interesting when not partaking in the culinary arts of fine food and drink.

I have been asked numerous times if I get hungry and thirsty. The tubal formula helps keep me hydrated, but does *nothing* to abate my hunger and thirst. My closest friends offer to let me smell their food and exotic drinks. This, in turn, is satisfying for me. I appreciate being with someone who is able to use all of their 10,000 taste buds and express the flavorful taste. I strive for stability while keeping a sense of humor through the challenges of not consuming food or drink orally.

I will wander into a bakery occasionally, just to savor the pleasant aroma wafting from the kitchen. On my birthday, I miss having a traditional birthday cake. My mother always made me a white cake with lemon filling. I would always get ill after eating a slice. Drinking A&W Root Beer from a frosty mug is also greatly missed. I do *not*, however, miss the complications that compounded my condition after eating or drinking.

With inner determination I am able to cook and bake, host parties, help with preparations, and appreciate the aroma of my home cooking. When I bake, it's cathartic. I have prepared mouth-watering pies just to watch my loved ones' eyes light up in happiness after savoring the taste.

The presentation of a beautiful table is important to me. It is the first step of visual appeal. I enjoy mixing textures of linens, dinnerware, flatware, and stemware with wisps of colors in designing a striking atmosphere. Centerpieces are a favorite craft I enjoy creating to complement the table setting and each occasion.

If I am not the hostess, I enjoy being included in dining excursions. I was nestled into a restaurant booth with several people who had ordered food and spirits. When I didn't order, I was told by a waitress, "You are taking up a spot." The merriment and laughter of everyone became an awkward hush after her remark. Friends asked the waitress and manager, "How can Rosie possibly be taking up space at a private table?" It didn't seem to make sense.

I had followed the written establishment rules. No entrance allowed if not wearing a shirt or shoes. Please seat yourself. Now I felt singled out. Where was I to go? Was I supposed to slide under the table? It would have been a rude action on my part to exit and go wait in the car for my friends to finish eating. I remained at the booth in silence. Forcing a smile, I held back a tsunami of emotions. I wanted to blurt them out, expressing frustration to the entire establishment: "I am starving! I truly desire that juicy hamburger, onion rings, taco salad, wild rice soup, and Texas toast they are having, that I can't." I didn't think I needed to explain my circumstances. I just wanted to visit with my friends, and feel part of the daily occurrence of dinner. I wanted to do more than exist. I wanted to live in the moment, without the impact of judgment.

Unfortunately, a few years later a similar scenario played out at a different restaurant location. I wish to fit in and participate in private and social events like everyone else. When that doesn't happen, I can cry heartfelt tears or aspire to dance in the rain and free my spirit. I do say a prayer that God's light will reach into their hearts with compassion, letting them realize that not everyone is able to eat, drink, and be merry in the same manner that most partake. I feel it is never wasted, taking up space to be in the presence of those you love to be with. I am grateful to still be alive to do so, and try to radiate thankfulness.

Most restaurant personnel have been kind to me. To those compassionate souls, I am grateful and thank you. I recall a polite restaurant owner asking to hear my story and then telling me, "You are beautiful inside and out." How compassionate his sincere remarks were; giving me comfort still to this day.

# REFRESHING
# MOISTURE

A dear friend stopped by to visit. We have been friends since we were in our teens. Like any pair of tried-and-true girlfriends, we have experienced many joys and trials together. She placed a gift bag next to my side. Bundled between tissue paper, I found an intricate sculpture with a purple design in the center of the glass. This art piece was in the form of a teardrop. She looked at me with tears welling in her brown eyes and explained, "I want you to know that when you shed tears of pain others cry with you."

Silence then filled the room with feelings of mutual respect and love for each other. What a comfort, to know that many people exude empathy. I have examined the delicate teardrop sculpture numerous times since that day. Each time, I imagine the warmth of love enveloping me.

"There is sacredness in tears. They are not the mark of weakness, but of power. They speak more eloquently than ten thousand tongues. They are the messengers of overwhelming grief, of deep contrition and of unspeakable love." —Washington Irving

I was outside examining water droplets encompassing thirsty cat-kins on a tree that had been planted in memory of my beloved father. I marveled how after a long winter, spring breathes new life all around us with moisturizing rebirth. What a great reminder that there is no life without water, hydrating nature and our human souls.

Friends also supply refreshing moisture to my spirit. Their hugs are physical healers. Precious children created and delivered artwork that I treasure. Others escorted me for a car excursion, a ride as the means to escape my confinement. A few moments to breathe fresh air and enjoy the beauty of pelicans gliding across quiet waters granted peace to en-velop my whole being. Phone calls, prayers, and messages of support, along with surprise visits from near and far, linger in my heart.

A caring friend sent me an attractive glass butterfly. I was listening to "How Great Thou Art" when I gazed at the multicolored butterfly wings and imagined flying to heaven. The musical arrangement was being performed by once-tiny fingers that I had taught to play melo-dies on ivory keyboards. Now mature hands mastered this inspirational song to perfection. Through an internet connection, I was gifted to watch him perform this soulful rendition for me.

In July 2015, the year's Miss Litchfield Watercade candidates were interviewed. When I read the interviews in the newspaper, it tugged at my heartstrings. They were asked to state the person they most admire and why. I was blown over when one young lady replied, "The person I admire most is Rosie Hartwig-Benson. She is strong-willed; she never gives up, and can do anything. I admire her because if she can do all of that, so can I." A dear girl of only seventeen years of age noticed my positivity and willful smile of endurance. When in pain, I don't always succeed in smiling, but I try to reflect thankfulness when embracing each new day.

She reserved seats for us to attend the coronation ceremony. She was crowned 1st Princess of Litchfield. It was a gratifying evening. She is now in college pursuing her degree. You never know who is touched by your situation. At the coronation, a lady approached me and told me I was an epitome of strength. I was touched with deep gratitude, and became teary-eyed when thanking her.

Not long ago, I gleaned wisdom after reading a handwritten letter sent to me from someone I had never met. When she heard of my circumstances, she composed her inner thoughts on how my story had enriched her life, telling her to never give up. I was having a fleeting moment of feeling flawed before reading her note. I reminded myself of what I should do: *Embrace you, Rosie.* I have learned that simple acts of kindness have the ability to change my whole day. I shouldn't be ashamed of my scars, or the extra tubal apparatus that helps keep me alive. They make me who I am. I am learning to be confident in my own skin, even the parts that make me stand out in a crowd. Beauty begins the moment I decide to embrace my imperfections. The rarity of a handwritten letter makes it a timeless, treasured keepsake. I plan to take the time to write more handwritten thoughts to acquaintances, instead of always sending emails.

A lady I had not seen in several years noticed me at a store and gasped, "You are alive, Rosie! I heard you had died." She squeezed my hand in thankfulness that I was still on this earth. Her enthusiasm and compassion made my day blessed. Amen, for sincere acts of love and the grace to have beaten the odds.

Life is a mixture of sunshine and rain, teardrops and laughter, pleasure and pain. We all face tribulations. When we go through those storms, let us remind ourselves that we have wings to fly to a brighter place by believing in the promise of a new tomorrow. The natural phenomenon of a rainbow appears after a storm, dispersing feelings of hope. May the gift of hope mingled with the sunshine rays of His faithful promises walk hand and hand with you throughout your journey.

# HIGH STANDARDS

While I lay bedridden, cocooned in the fluffy warmth of flannel bed sheets, I had fleeting thoughts of high heels. Days previously, my physical therapist had asked me what my goals were. I explained, "To wear heels and to master walking in them." The PT's expression was of surprise. She knew I was feeble, and had all I could do to muster up enough strength to get out of bed, even with assistance. She exclaimed, "Rosie, together we will make that happen!" I set my aspirations to high standards.

Inside my mother's treasured photo album is a photograph of her little Rosie, hanging wet doll clothes on a reachable clothesline. Mom told me I occupied many hours washing and drying doll clothes in the summer sun, always while wearing her heels. What little girl doesn't like to clunk around in their mother's high heels, claiming her femininity at an early age?

I set about the task of physical therapy with diligence. Many tears of anguish were experienced in each session. Enduring through the rebuilding, muscle-strengthening exercises was exhausting and a challenge.

Have you ever noticed a wildflower growing in a crack of a cement driveway, and wondered how it could survive in such dry conditions and with such sparse soil to bloom? I thought of myself as that tiny flower. I was still alive to hope and grow in adverse conditions. It made me determined that my goal was attainable. I *was* going to succeed.

After spending too much of the past twenty years wearing open-back, stiff hospital gowns, the very thought of leaving my home to go shopping for heels and perhaps a pretty, lace-embroidered top was consuming me. To elevate myself to a new level of positivity, I dreamed of such an excursion happening in the near future.

Several years ago, a dear girlfriend picked me up for a road trip to celebrate life. We decided to go to Macy's department store. We spent almost two hours trying on different styles and colors of high heels. We were turning heads with our excited hoots of, "Oh, look at this one!" and gasps when locating another style that we hadn't noticed during our quick scan a second ago. There are many shoes made for comfort, but when a woman puts on a six-inch heel, she transforms into Cinderella. In that instant, all need for comfort is forgotten.

The helpful sales lady told us a certain designer footwear line would be going on sale the following week. We giggled and jokingly replied, "We will be back to purchase one of each kind!" Who doesn't like a good sale? We narrowed our selection down to four elegant pairs, and placed the high heel finalists' photos on my Sweet Conclusions Area Voices blog. Women from hither and yon voted on their favorite style, no doubt helping all mankind.

Ladies in a shoe department can have the time of their life just trying on stiletto heels. I recommend this free form of relaxation, and the wow-factor experience of shopping. I left the department store happy and stress-free, with a smile from ear to ear. Now on the wings of my hopeful dream, I was able to fly with new confidence while recalling this gratifying escapade.

I felt giving myself a goal with reward was an avenue of understanding the validity of my emotions. It was my way of feeling revitalized after enduring the bedridden struggles of waking up and strengthening my weakened muscles, a form of loving myself more.

After persevering and not giving up on my dream, sixteen months later I reached my goal. Taken on a date, I proudly wore black velveteen ankle-strap high heels with a beautiful lace top and pencil skirt. Feeling totally feminine, I am certain I understand how Cinderella must have felt going to the ball.

After being trapped in my own little corner, in my own little room, finally being able to flee into the outside world was exhilarating. As an added bonus, no hospital gowns were in sight.

I was home long before midnight, and not losing my shoe I didn't become a fairy-tale princess. But in my mind, I had been a queen for a few hours. I recalled a phrase from *The Wizard of Oz*: "You always had the power my dear; you just had to learn it for yourself."

# SHARE THAT SMILE

One morning, a maintenance man arrived at my home to fix a household problem. When I opened the door, I greeted him with a smile and said, "Welcome; it appears to be warmer outside this morning."

He looked at me like I was eccentric, at best, to say a crisp morning in Minnesota was a few degrees warmer. His reply was curt: "I have already had a wild morning—and it is only Monday."

The feline of this household always checks out a visitor. I was surprised when her back arched, with the fur standing on end. He also noticed and snickered, "That cat is agitated by my presence."

He went about his job. I heard tools drop a couple of times, and deep audible sighs when he went down a flight of stairs to fetch more supplies.

Finishing the job, he presented me with an invoice. I stated, "Thank you for your promptness in completing this task quickly. I hope the rest of your day and week goes more smoothly."

He left and closed the door. A few seconds later, the doorbell chimed. I again greeted him with a smile. This time he returned a smile, and with a pleasant speaking tone said, "While going to the truck, I happened to notice it does seem to be warmer today. Thank you for pointing this out, and for sharing your smile. If you have more maintenance issues, give me a call."

Long story short, we all go through multiple issues in our daily life. Health problems, pain, stress, personal and financial issues, loss of a loved one, long hours at our place of employment, etc. Let's build each other up, taking the time to reflect on finding the positives in the day and then cherishing them. I have always found it is easier to explain my smile then why I am sad. There is always something to be grateful for.

A loved one attached an endearing note to my bedside lamp: "Love you, Rosie, keep smiling." I am reminded that I am fortunate to have scars and feel pain. My perseverance, faith, gratitude, and courage help instill peace when I go through overwhelming trials. I have survived adversity with a smile on my face.

Surprise someone with a smile and infuse joy. It might make their day suddenly appear worthwhile, with endless echoes.

# DON'T SPELL IT, FEEL IT

I had been anticipating attending a special wedding for over a year. After undergoing another surgery, I was persistent while working on physical therapy exercises to be able to achieve this goal. I was filled with exuberance when my son and I entered the venue.

I was enthralled by the gracious innocence of a two-year-old flower girl kneeling. She was wearing butterfly wings over her beautiful white gown. In her auburn hair were strands of multicolored flowers. I shivered and felt instant goosebumps all over my skin. I reached for my camera to capture her gracefulness.

In that moment, I didn't hear the loud barrage of noise in the background of the venue. I was enveloped in silent peacefulness. God was revealing to me why my endurance to attend this event had been granted. I sensed it was for me to be touched by this butterfly angel. Love surrounded me in new levels with overflowing purity.

Love can be understood and learned with more clarity through children. I also noticed a glowing love between the bride and groom. I thought of when Piglet asked Winnie the Pooh, "How do you spell love?" Pooh responded, "You don't spell it, you feel it."

I agree with Pooh. I need to be in tune with my surroundings to feel being encompassed with the gratefulness of love.

Continuing to watch this young girl kneeling, I was reminded of a quote: "Fall on your knees and grow there, because when life gives you more than you can stand, kneel and pray."

What an important message: "Fall on your knees and grow there." The storms in my life do not need to overwhelm me, if I give my worries to God for validation. I am sustained by entrusting my life and future into His hands, and will be rejuvenated.

# GRATITUDE

I love spending solitary time amid the grandeur of nature. The first rays of morning sun penetrated my body with warmth. Standing in close proximity to a hummingbird feeder, Mister Hummer arrived. He didn't seem to mind that I was invading his personal space. Viewing his iridescent gorget, I was transfixed, thankful I was able to capture his incredible form. I was given an enthralling nature experience. With no window pane between us, it was similar in experiencing fireworks on the 4th of July, captivating me with stunning beauty.

Continuing to explore the simplicity of nature, I noticed a water droplet on a bough. I discovered an intricate spider's silk thread woven through the moisture. Dangling from the bottom of the thread was a tiny water droplet, wavering in the wind. I examined the fineness of the spider's craftsmanship with the camera lens on full zoom. It conveyed to me that although not always visible to the human eye, I also have been hanging on by a thread. Given extreme challenges, my journey has proceeded down a different path than I had envisioned for my future. Entwined threads of faith, patience, grace, and fortitude have prevailed. These threads have cleansed my tears, while holding me securely to keep me from faltering.

Strolling along a flowing river bank on a carefree afternoon, I was startled when I heard large wings flapping. To my surprise, a majestic bald eagle was sweeping over the cool water, where it latched into a fish. The eagle's massive wingspan appeared to be seven feet when he soared to a sturdy branch. Atop the tree, it reigned over wooded terrain like a white-headed king sitting on a throne. The eagle's yellow eyes glistened in the sunlight. I was awestruck by this rare occurrence, and its mighty physique. It made me think back to the meaningful lyrics in the song "On Eagle's Wings": "He will raise you up on eagle's wings." That devotional composition added a special touch at both of my parents' funeral services. Whenever I hear the melody, it makes the hair on my arms stand on end. I started humming the chorus while watching the eagle. It left me in a spellbound state of mind until I sauntered back to the car.

A month later, I had the fantastic opportunity to view America's national symbol resting atop an eyrie. It is amazing to ponder the determination needed to build such a massive nesting site.

I am drawn to God's splendor each time I commune with nature. For me, it is similar to stepping into an old slipper, or wrapping a favorite old shawl around my shoulders. It always fits, and gives me incredible comfort. I gain a new lease on the immense importance of everyday treasures surrounding me, and a better understanding of His perfection.

# EPILOGUE

The flower that blooms in adversity is the rarest and most beautiful of all. A dainty Rose, whose petals became jaded through the trials of life and numerous surgeries, has persisted and survived.

My dreams were interrupted during long periods of being bedridden. Delicate petals wilted from lack of hydration and painful exhaustion. Miraculous new petals have emerged after time and renewed stamina. I realize that faith, hope, courage, and love are like drops of water giving a wilted flower enough strength to revive itself.

While healing with uniqueness, my petal layers are now different. Life still has its challenges, but I am stronger in spirit. When dealing with the obstacles of tubal procedures required every twelve weeks for survival, I dream differently. I see through painful veils with a clarified focus, and embrace each second, entrusting that whatever path is destined for me will be victorious. Gratitude always turns what we have into enough.

My evenings are often spent in silence, reflecting. It is in those moments that I hear God whisper in my ear. "Rosie, I have plans for your future. You are loved. Let that promise be enough for you to sing a new song. Your story isn't over yet."

I inhale the simplest of joys: a baby cooing, the luxurious feeling of a new pair of socks, the fresh smell of air-dried linens, the comforting purr of a kitten, watching a rose unfold, a bird's sweet melody, being in the same room with loved ones, feasting my eyes upon an incandescent sunset, searching for a heart-shape on an unbeaten path, watching the rerun virtues of small-town American life portrayed on the *Andy Griffith Show*, or capturing moments with a camera. These things, among other small pleasures, make me sparkle and shine and reflect appreciation.

I have been blessed with glimpses of the wonders of heaven's peace, and floated with my guardian angels. It is not yet my time to be in heaven. I am to keep being faithful, loving, and here for my beloved son—and perhaps for you, the person reading this.

Remind yourself you are loved by the one who created us. If you are fortunate enough to have someone sitting next to you, tell them what they mean to you. If you love them to the moon and back, express yourself. Life is short. Don't wait until tomorrow.

God bless us as we each face our struggles with faith, courage, and grace. A positive person sees a promise, an opportunity, in each difficulty and in each new day. A wonderful blessing is either seen or unseen, but the blessings are always there if we seek to be open to them, and live life to our fullest potential.

While composing this last chapter, God's radiating sunlight painted a magnificent, feather-shaped rainbow on the wall. I felt angelic spirits encompass my surroundings with tranquility, and refuel my soul with reverence.

Amidst those whispers, I have a guided, humble perspective of my circumstances. I know His prism of rainbow love is caressing me, calling my name, and strengthening my voyage. My smile radiates serenity with His grace.

Embrace each possibility along your journey. Take the time to stop and smell the roses. Examine each petal of distinction, and rejoice in the miracle of daily life.

Love with abundance. Tomorrow's blessings are patiently waiting.

# ACKNOWLEDGMENTS

Life's joys and tangles unravel more easily with help from family, friends, medical professionals, and God's power to restore. Thank you for your love, support, and prayers.

Be blessed,
*Rosie*

# ABOUT THE AUTHOR

Rosie Hartwig-Benson is a native of Minnesota. Receiving a college degree in design and merchandising, she worked in the realms of retail before becoming an office manager at a chiropractic clinic. Years later, she became a mother and decided to foster young children's growth through Rosie's Daycare.

Rosie is a gentle and kind spirit filled with a positive perspective of her battle with gastroparesis complications. She finds strength during her moment to moment health struggles by embracing the simple pleasures in life. Capturing Minnesota's four seasons with a camera and creating art designs gives her life zest.

Nothing makes her happier than spending time with loved ones.

## YOU CAN VISIT ROSIE ONLINE AT:

rosa136.wixsite.com/sweetconclusions
sweetconclusions.areavoices.com
facebook.com/SweetConclusions

CPSIA information can be obtained
at www.ICGtesting.com
Printed in the USA
FFOW03n1757280318
46016588-46912FF